Quilting
on the Go!

Jessica Alexandrakis

Search Press

A QUARTO BOOK

Published in 2013 by
Search Press Ltd
Wellwood
North Farm Road
Tunbridge Wells
Kent TN2 3DR

ISBN: 978-1-84448-902-2

Conceived, designed and produced by
Quarto Publishing plc
The Old Brewery
6 Blundell Street
London N7 9BH

QUAR.EPQ

Senior editor: Katie Crous
Copy editor: Ruth Patrick
Art director: Caroline Guest
Art editor and designer: Jackie Palmer
Photographers: Ned Witrogen (steps),
    Phil Wilkins (stills), Nicki Dowey
    and Simon Pask (lifestyle)
Illustrators: John Woodcock, Kuo Kang Chen
Picture researcher: Sarah Bell
Proofreader: Sarah Hoggett
Creative director: Moira Clinch
Publisher: Paul Carslake

Colour separation by Modern Age Repro
House Ltd, Hong Kong
Printed in China by Hung Hing Off-Set
Printing Co Ltd

Contents

About this book

Here you will find everything you need to get started with English Paper Piecing (EPP). The book is organised into five chapters, starting with tools and techniques and progressing through to projects and a collection of patterns guaranteed to inspire beginners and more experienced quilters. Finally, there's a section of graph paper at the end for drafting your own designs.

Chapter 1: Getting ready,
pages 14–33
Whether you're paper piecing at home or on the go, this chapter tells you everything you need to get started, including a master class in combining pattern and colour to make pleasing quilt tops.

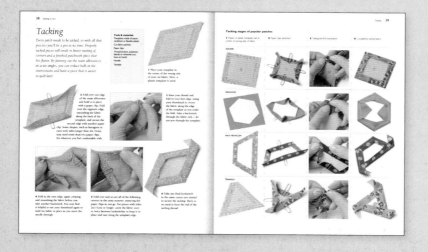

Chapter 2: Starting to sew,
pages 34–57
All the techniques you need at your fingertips, from tricks for cutting fabric to troubleshooting while stitching, and a complete guide on how to finish your quilt.

Chapter 3: The projects, *pages 58–103*

A range of easy to intermediate projects let you put into practice the techniques you learned in chapter 2.

Measurements

Since the vast majority of quilters use imperial measurements for cutting and sewing the pieces of their quilts, all measurements throughout this book are provided in imperial followed by metric conversions in brackets. Do not swap between the two systems when cutting and sewing. However, even if you work in the imperial system, you may sometimes find the metric conversions useful, such as for buying fabric.

Everything you will need laid out neatly to give an overview of what's required

Pattern pieces used in the project

Clear step-by-step photographs

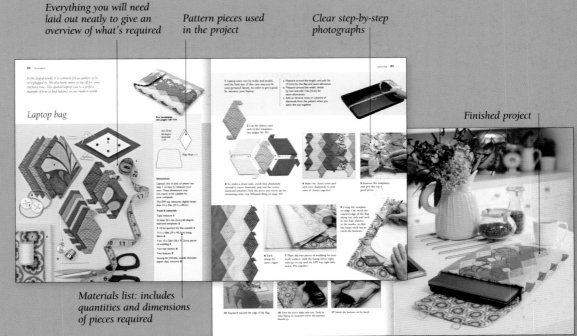

Finished project

Materials list: includes quantities and dimensions of pieces required

Chapter 4: English paper-piecing patterns, *pages 104–125*

Core shapes used in paper piecing are explored here: diamonds, stars, hexagons, squares – see how shapes can be combined, tessellated and worked in different colourways to make scores of wonderful patterns.

Base grid in an easy-to-read line format and in colour to match the photo sample

Piecing sequence: graphics indicate the order in which to sew the pieces together.

Key

- – = start sewing here
2 = order to sew
- → = direction to sew

Variations demonstrate how pieces can be arranged in different colourways or different orientations to show some of the possibilities available to the designer.

Stitched sample

Chapter 5: Paper-piecing resources *pages 126–139*

This chapter contains some useful tools: actual-size templates for the paper pieces used in the projects; pattern templates for the shoulder bag, small pouch and laptop case; a stack of ready-to-photocopy or scan graph-paper grids to let you create your own perfectly precise patterns.

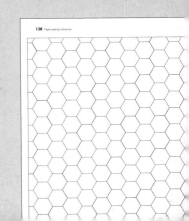

Projects preview

The projects shown here are featured in Chapter 3, pages 58–103, with clear step-by-step guidance for making your own. Replicate the designs exactly or use them as inspiration and add your own twist to make a project that's truly unique.

Tiny sewing kit, pages 60–63

Travel quilt, pages 100–103

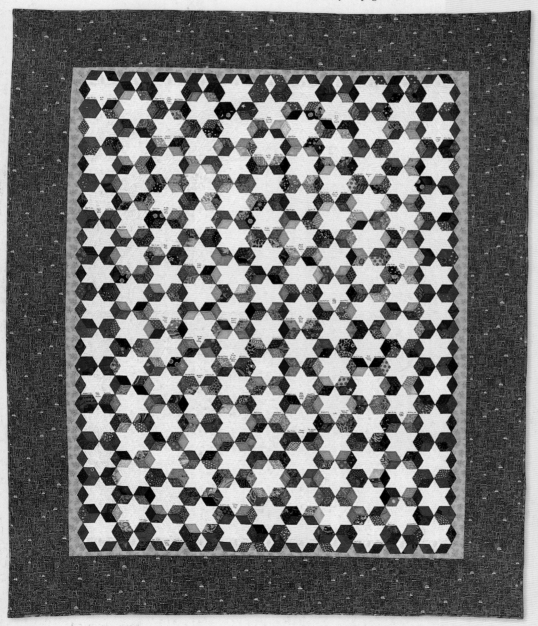

Shoulder bag, pages 72–79

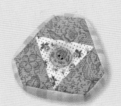

Pincushion, pages 68–71

Photo frame, pages 96–99

Hexagon cushion,
pages 64–67

Tanuki stripe throw,
pages 92–95

Small pouch,
pages 80–83

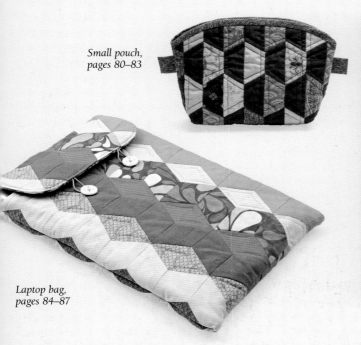

Laptop bag,
pages 84–87

Falling stars baby quilt,
pages 88–91

My world of English paper piecing

The internet is full of creative inspiration — people crafting, sewing, blogging and sharing. There is a healthy and vibrant community of crafters online. However, in real life we don't get to see a lot of people making things any more. Crafting in public is one way to stand out in the community and tell the world, 'Yes, it's okay to slow down. Things made by hand are still valued.' Whether you quilt alone or with friends, having a hand-piecing project ready to carry with you will let you make use of all those moments away from home that would otherwise have been wasted.

WHY I LOVE THIS CRAFT

If I have free time, I want to be quilting because it relaxes me. With English paper piecing, the stitches are simple and repetitive, and the patterns easy to follow, making it a great activity for meditative stress relief.

My relationship with English paper piecing came partly from necessity and partly from curiosity. I am one of those people who doesn't like to sit idle – I need to keep my hands moving. My first English paper-pieced quilt started on a trip to Japan in 2007. I needed something portable that wouldn't bother the surrounding passengers on the 14-hour flight. I also didn't want to bring too many tools with me, leaving precious luggage space for the treasures I would bring home (fabric!). I had seen a photo on the internet of a charm quilt made from hundreds of different-coloured diamonds stitched into stars and I was intrigued. I started piecing 1½in (4cm) diamonds into coloured stars with an interlocking white background and I was hooked: I pieced in the airport, on the plane, at my host's kitchen table as we talked throughout my stay. I even went through her fabric and cut some pink diamonds to add to my quilt, to stand as a physical reminder of the time we spent together.

Even though I have made many different types of quilts, I find myself returning time and again to English paper piecing because it gives me a chance during a busy day to unwind and be alone with my thoughts. Somehow, when I'm hand piecing, I always feel happier, more in tune with myself and more satisfied because I am creating.

PATCHWORK IN THE PARK

This get-together in New York's Central Park was the perfect day out for the NYC Modern Quilt Guild. What could be better than hand sewing on picnic blankets under the trees?

FOLLOW YOUR INTUITION

This book features the methods I've found work best for me after years of trial and error, talking with friends and blogging about English paper piecing (EPP). If you find a method or a step that feels more natural to you, do it your way. The goal is to enjoy the process of quiltmaking and to have beautiful items as the outcome.

Quilting in a digital age

If you are new to quilting you might not notice, but if you've been around a while, it's pretty clear to see that quilting has changed a lot in the last five to ten years. As technology has changed our lives, quilters have been quick to adapt it to their needs, and new resources, shops and communities have popped up all over the place.

One of the biggest additions to quilting in the digital age is the introduction of blogs written by ordinary people about the quilts that they make. Bloggers can share patterns, tutorials, photos of finished projects or works in progress, the stories behind the quilts and other useful information such as reviews of books and quilting tools. The internet has become a place that quilters can turn to in order to discover techniques and find inspiration to start their own projects.

Bloggers and their readers often become friends through the exchange of comments and emails, and this personal connection makes the experience of writing and reading blogs more enjoyable. I think the support of 'Blogland' has helped me focus my creative energy and become a productive, happy quilter.

There are also countless websites that provide instructional videos or a place to upload photographs, and quilters have flocked to these sites to learn, share and find new ideas for their craft.

Creating communities online

While many quilters head to the internet to gain knowledge or inspiration, still others log in to the many communities that have formed over the past few years. Platforms such as Flickr and Twitter make it easy to jump in on conversations and not only share what you've made, but also get feedback almost instantly. This speed of communication between friends or total strangers is one of the things that is propelling the current online movement of quilters. No longer do you have to wait until the monthly guild meeting in your neighbourhood to show off what you've made; nowadays you make it, post it and instantly know what people think of it. It is tremendously motivating to be part of such communities.

One of the best aspects of the online quilting community is the accepting atmosphere. If you want

Sharing through blogs

Quilt blogs share photos and stories about the author's life as well as his or her journey in quilt making. They often openly engage their readers in conversations (read the comments!) and invite or encourage readers to join Quilt-alongs, blog-hops or challenges. Blogs may also have links to other creative sites, tutorials and quilt shops.

Many blogs have tabs across the top where you can learn more about the author, look at completed quilts, view a collection of tutorials and see other online projects in which the blogger has participated.

A sidebar may list other blogs that the blogger enjoys reading, which is helpful in leading you to new sites and quilters.

ENCOURAGING RESULTS
This Diamond Star Quilt by Lesly Wade-Woolley was one of the first finished projects from my '60-degree Diamond EPP Quilt-along', which is still up and running.

to try a technique, you will likely find several examples or tutorials out there and many people sharing 'their way' to do it. As a quilter (new or experienced) you have the freedom to read them all, ask questions and then forge ahead with whichever method is a good fit for your personal style. There is less criticism and it is a less intimidating forum than traditional, face-to-face quilting communities. There is an atmosphere of trying and learning together.

Online quilt-alongs

Another great trend is online 'quilt-alongs', where one person posts an idea, theme or pattern, and invites others to join in and form a group where they can encourage each other as they all work on the same project. In 2010, after sharing my love of 60-degree diamonds with several friends, I started a '60-degree Diamond EPP Quilt-along' on my blog and on Flickr. More than 100 people joined to show their love of English paper-pieced diamonds, ask and answer questions, and share photos of their progress. Thousands of diamonds were cut and tacked, millions of stitches were taken and, slowly but surely, some truly amazing quilts were made – see the quilt pictured on the opposite page, above.

Modern Quilt Guild

Quilters are typically social beings, so it was no big surprise that the community online spurred on the creation of real-life quilt guilds. The Modern Quilt Guild started as an online phenomenon, where people could create online guilds for their hometowns and see if there were any other quilters locally who would like to join. If there was enough interest in having in-person gatherings, the quilters would discuss the possibility via the internet and then find a physical location to hold meetings. After a few years, many local modern quilt guilds have sprung up all over the world. Some have monthly meetings, and most also have an online component, either a blog or website, where members can share information any time, anywhere. I am a proud member of the NYC Modern Quilt Guild, where the motivation and encouragement from the online

quilt movement is present in a real, live energy that fills the room each time we get together. The thrill of being part of such an inspiring group of quilters is truly amazing. For more information, or to see if there is a chapter of the Modern Quilt Guild in your area, please visit themodernquiltguild.com.

Internet as a place to shop

Undoubtedly, the internet is a wonderful place to go shopping for quilt fabric and notions. From large, professional quilt shops to small, home-based stores on Etsy, it's possible to find anything you are looking for on the internet. For a list of some online quilt shops, see the Resources section on page 140.

Mobile devices

Quilters can take the internet on the go with them as well. There are many iPad and mobile phone apps that quilters use, such as Evernote to store and sort design ideas, and even apps to calculate fabric quantities.

Don't forget that the camera on your phone is a great tool for recording quilt projects or inspiration, which you can instantly upload to any of the online communities. You can also take pictures of your current project and refer to them while you're away from home. This is useful when trying to match fabric colours while shopping, or to remember your pattern while quilting on the go.

THE GUILD COMMUNITY
Many of the branches of the Modern Quilt Guild maintain blogs for their groups. In a group blog, all members of the guild are able to contribute, and posts range from recaps of meetings, progress reports on group projects, local quilt shows and events, and individual member projects. If any members maintain individual blogs, they are often listed in a sidebar.

chapter

1

Getting ready

Are you ready to get started? Then it's time to find out about all the various tools and notions used in English paper piecing, as well as how to choose that all-important fabric and learn about other preparations that will help to put your project in motion.

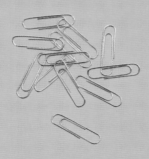

Choosing tools and notions

We are lucky to have access to a wide range of options when it comes to tools and notions. Once you start quilting, or if you've been doing it for a while, you will discover which ones you like and which you don't. It may take some trial and error, but once you find what works best for you, the right tools help get the job done more smoothly and definitely make it more enjoyable.

Fabric

If you want your quilted project to last, it is important to pay attention to the quality of the fabrics you use. The best for English paper piecing (EPP) are 100 per cent cotton quilting-weight fabrics, because they are durable enough to withstand being handled over and over as you cut, tack and piece your block and manoeuvre your blocks into a quilt top. For a detailed explanation of how to choose fabrics, turn to page 20.

Templates

While it is possible to trace and cut out all of your EPP templates from paper that you have at home, it is much more efficient to order pre-cut packages of paper or plastic templates. Templates can be used repeatedly and some types work better than others, depending on the pattern requirements and the angles that need to be sewn. The various options for templates are discussed in more detail on page 32.

Cotton piecing thread

Wadding

Wadding is the soft layer that goes between a quilt top and the backing fabric. Waddings can be made from cotton, bamboo, polyester and even recycled plastic bottles. There are many popular brands of cotton or cotton/polyester blends, but no matter what you choose, a low-loft wadding, which is thinner and less fluffy, works best.

Thread (tacking and piecing)

Thread used to tack your fabric to the templates can be any type (cotton, polyester or blends) but it should not be darker than the fabric so it won't show through on the front. Thread used to piece your templates together should be 100 per cent cotton. Use a thread colour that matches, or is similar to, the fabric you are piecing. Multicoloured units can be pieced with a neutral such as beige or grey. When piecing darks to lights, or other contrasting fabrics, choose a thread that closely matches one of the fabrics (for example, use red or white thread to piece red and white shapes together).

Polyester blend tacking thread

Cutting tools

You may already have some of the items featured here in your craft or sewing kit, but in the long term it will pay off to have a good selection of cutting tools at your disposal.

Quilter's acrylic ruler, rotary cutter and mat

These tools have become very popular with quilters as they allow for quick, easy and accurate cutting and measuring in one step. Along with a ruler to cut long strips of fabric (a 6 x 24in [15 x 60cm] ruler is a popular size for this), smaller rulers or specialist shapes can come in handy when cutting the shapes needed for your EPP project. If you are looking for a good acrylic ruler, make sure to find one with clear 45- and 60-degree angle markings.

Craft knife or old rotary blade

If you will be cutting your templates from paper or cardstock, don't use your fabric scissors. Instead, use an acrylic ruler and mat with a craft knife or an old rotary cutting blade that you designate only for paper.

Fabric scissors

Any sharp pair of scissors designated only for fabric will do the job just as well as specialist fabric scissors. You can either trace your template and cut around it including seam allowance, or just hold up a template as you cut the fabric, estimating a sufficient seam allowance. If you are taking your EPP project with you on a holiday or other long trip, it may be more practical to take scissors rather than an 18 x 12in (46 x 30cm) cutting mat and ruler.

Ergonomic rotary cutter

1in (28mm) blade rotary cutter

1¾in (45mm) blade rotary cutter

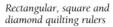

Thread cutter

Thread cutter or small scissors

A thread cutter is a small blade encased in metal or plastic that you can pull your thread against to cut it. This is faster than using scissors, and some thread cutters can be worn as a pendant around the neck, making it always easily accessible. Another option is a small pair of scissors just for cutting threads.

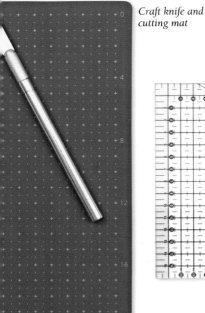

Craft knife and cutting mat

Rectangular, square and diamond quilting rulers

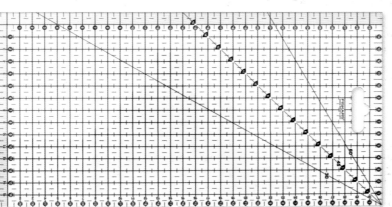

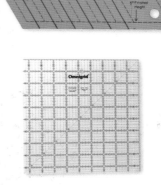

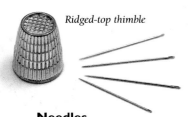

Ridged-top thimble

Standard thimble

Open-topped thimble

Leather thimble with metal disc

Needles

Needles are a very personal item for each quilter. The length of the shaft, size of the eye and thickness of the needle all play a part in how comfortable they are to hold and how easy they are to use. I prefer to tack, piece and finish my quilts with a #10 between, which is short, sharp and thick. If you are new to hand piecing, try out a few types of needles until you find one that feels comfortable to you.

Thimble

Hand piecing is much more comfortable when you get used to wearing a thimble. There are many varieties available and it's best to test out a few different types until you find one that feels good on your finger. They come in a wide assortment of materials – metal, rubber, leather and even adhesive-backed plastic dots.

Needle threaders

Wax

Quilting wax is used to coat the thread to make it stronger as you hand piece. Thread can get worn and frayed from travelling repeatedly through the layers of fabric or from friction against the eye of the needle. Running your thread through the wax each time you rethread your needle will help you get a few more inches of uninterrupted sewing from each thread. It also helps prevent the thread from tangling.

Needle threader

These small tools have a thin loop of wire at one end. Insert the wire in the eye of the needle, then pass the thread through the wire loop and pull the wire out again. Your needle will be threaded without having to strain your eyes. Even if you don't usually use a needle threader, keep one in your EPP sewing kit for help in low-light situations.

Paper clips

Paper clips are useful for holding the fabric to your template as you tack. Standard-size, uncoated clips work best.

Straight pins and curved quilter's safety pins

Straight pins are used to attach an EPP top to the border fabric before it is appliquéd into place. Curved quilter's safety pins are used for tacking.

Temporary spray adhesive

Small quilting projects can be quilted much more quickly with the help of a fabric-safe adhesive (sometimes called basting spray or spray baste) that temporarily holds the three layers of the project together so that it can be quilted. No pins or tacking thread required.

Clear plastic pouch

As your project progresses, it helps to have a clear plastic bag or pouch to hold the puzzle pieces until you can join them. Zip-up packaging from bedding or other household textiles, or even from some types of clothing, can be repurposed for project storage. Remember to include a card with your name and contact information in case you accidentally leave it at the car repair shop or dentist's office!

Mobile phone or digital camera

This may seem like a strange tool to add to the list, but try taking a photo of your project in progress and storing it on your phone or camera. Then when you are out and about, piecing somewhere away from home, you can refer back to it to check colour placement or remind yourself which piece to stitch next. It's also useful when people ask what you're making and you can show them a photo of something bigger than the two templates you are currently stitching together.

Sewing kit

Having all of your small tools and notions together with your cut patches and templates makes it possible to take your project with you or move your sewing comfortably from room to room. More details on building a travel tool kit can be found on page 30.

A good set of fingernails

Don't underestimate the importance of a good set of fingernails! They are especially useful when tacking the fabric to your templates, and finger pressing the folds or running your nail over a crease can give you a crisp line to stitch on later.

Fabric

English paper piecing is a great way to show off your eye for fabrics or your abundant stash. The pieces are small, so even the tiniest novelty prints can be highlighted and the smallest scraps become useful. If you prefer an intuitive approach, use a large variety of prints along with one fabric that acts as an anchor to tie them together, and watch as a stunning quilt effortlessly designs itself.

For EPP, you can use 100 per cent cotton fabrics from anywhere: new, gifted, thrifted, swapped, scavenged or your family's cast-off clothing. (I've been known to be especially attentive to any signs of wear on my husband's shirts and point out even the smallest tear – hoping he'll say I can have it for fabric). So long as it is relatively close to quilting-weight cotton and can be pre-washed, it's fair game.

STORYTELLING

The fabric I use has its own memories, making the final quilted project more special. I know who I was with when I bought it, or what I had originally intended it for. Scraps used from other projects add more layers of memory and more stories to tell. The story in the fabric is like a personal scrapbook.

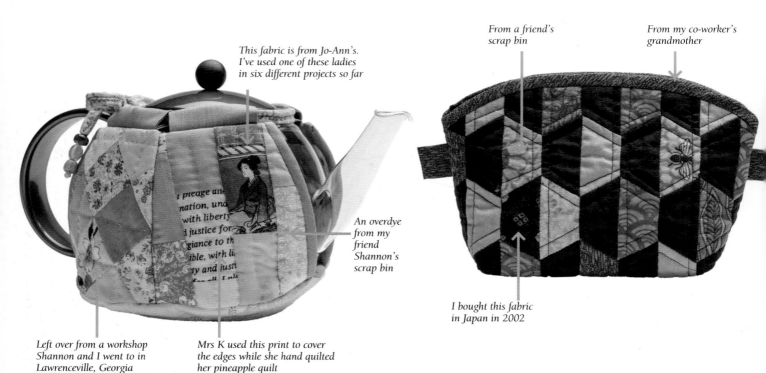

Lexi gave me this

I got this in Kyoto in '99

Left over from Zoe's quilt

The Atlanta guild made blocks for Radine using this fabric

This fabric is from Jo-Ann's. I've used one of these ladies in six different projects so far

An overdye from my friend Shannon's scrap bin

From a friend's scrap bin

From my co-worker's grandmother

I bought this fabric in Japan in 2002

Left over from a workshop Shannon and I went to in Lawrenceville, Georgia

Mrs K used this print to cover the edges while she hand quilted her pineapple quilt

Fabric acquisition guide

Acquiring fabric is one of the best parts of quilt making. Whether you buy fabric online or in person at a brick-and-mortar quilt shop, or inherit, trade or upcycle something into patches for your current project, the fabrics you choose to sew with can express who you are and what you liked at the time you made that quilt. Here are some of the ways to build your stash:

- **Visit your local shops** Depending on where you live, you may be able to find fabric for sale in a variety of shops. Independent quilt shops not only offer a selection of fabrics that reflect that shop's personality, but they are usually staffed with quilters and sewers who will eagerly assist you in matching, choosing and planning your project. With commerce increasingly switching to online, we don't know how long these physical quilt shops will be around, so I encourage you to support them as much as you can. Even if your fabric tastes differ from what the shop carries, you can still support them by purchasing notions, tools, books and other basics. A list of shops can be found in the Resources on page 140.
- **Scour online resources** When you want a specific fabric that you saw another quilter using on a blog, or you're following a particular designer's new seasonal releases, the most convenient place to shop is on the internet. Several blogs have links to popular fabric shops on their sidebars, and a few even put out weekly lists of the shops that are having sales. Although most shops charge for delivery, many offer reduced charges for purchases over a certain amount.

- **Finding freebies** Don't forget that there are many free or inexpensive ways to build your stash, including trading fabric with friends, participating in online swaps and being lucky enough to receive fabric from someone who is no longer quilting. Both my grandmother and a friend's grandmother passed down their stashes to me when they cleaned out their closets and decided to pursue other hobbies. There were some excellent vintage finds in both closets!
- **Second-hand treasures** Charity and second-hand shops can also be sources of interesting fabric to add to your projects. Wash any upcycled fabric well before you take apart the garment (to prevent unravelling), and cut out any areas that are stained, worn thin or attached to interfacing.
- **Cotton bed sheets** 100 per cent cotton bed sheets can make great quilt backings – be sure to check that the weave of the fabric is not too close to quilt through. Sheets and pillowcases may also be an inexpensive way to build your stash of solids and neutrals, or offer some interesting prints.

When deciding how much fabric to buy, consider how you plan to use it. Fat quarters and pre-cuts are a great way to build a stash or add variety to a project, but when you choose your background or constant fabric, it's a good idea to buy all of it at the same time. See page 37 for calculating fabric quantities depending on the size and shape of the templates you'll use.

Pre-washing

You should pre-wash all of your fabric, even scraps gifted, found, purchased or reclaimed. I wash even pre-cut fabric such as jelly rolls and layer cakes. Once you cut into it, the fabric becomes a scrap that you may use somewhere else. If you don't wash your fabric first, you run into the problem of not knowing what's washed and what isn't.

Use lingerie bags for your small scraps (anything smaller than a fat quarter) and toss them in with other larger pieces of fabric. I always wash fabric separately from clothes and other household laundry (I learned that lesson the hard way – I had a beautiful white print tablecloth that now has a yellow tint), and I always throw in one or two dye-catching cloths that suck the excess dye from the wash water. Sort into lights and darks and wash bold colours separately.

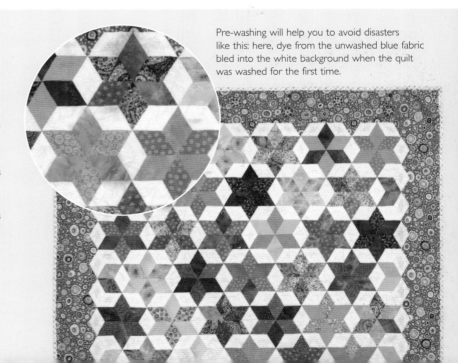

Pre-washing will help you to avoid disasters like this: here, dye from the unwashed blue fabric bled into the white background when the quilt was washed for the first time.

Choosing fabric for your project

Manufacturers' collections are great because they automatically go together, but don't just stop there.

- **Edit out from a collection** Don't use all the fabrics; focus on just a few (see patterns on pages 111 and 113). If there are several colours in the collection, try choosing just three to focus the palette. You might want to choose all cool or all warm colours, or play around with the colour wheel (see page 27) to see what combinations are possible.
- **Build from a collection** Add in stash fabrics that 'go' with the collection fabrics – the more, the better. Try to choose stash fabrics that are lighter or darker shades of the same colours, including solids, or add in a bold novelty print to liven things up or a neutral to calm them down.
- **Mix collections!** Often collections that come from the same manufacturer, designer or season will be similar enough that you can join them in really pleasing arrangements.

Buy fabrics and save fabrics that you love, then use them repeatedly. I have one cheater print (of Japanese ladies) that I found in 2002 at a large chain store. I have cut from this fabric and added a piece to six different projects. Your descendants will love spotting and solving puzzles like that decades from now.

EDITING DOWN AND BUILDING UP

Editing down a collection can provide the perfect opportunity for building it back up again with fabrics from your own stash, as was done here with a Moda collection.

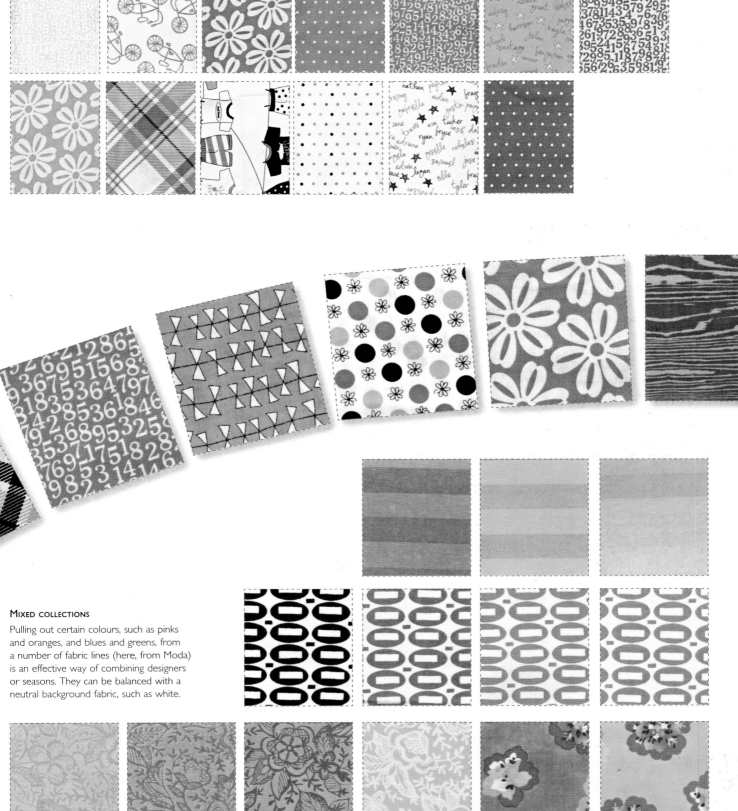

MIXED COLLECTIONS

Pulling out certain colours, such as pinks and oranges, and blues and greens, from a number of fabric lines (here, from Moda) is an effective way of combining designers or seasons. They can be balanced with a neutral background fabric, such as white.

Combining colours and patterns

Your fabrics look great all freshly pressed, but it is important to put some thought and time into how they will look once you cut them, tack away a seam allowance and join them with their new friends. Some multicoloured prints that seemed to be so bold lose their voice when they are cut up and the background colour takes over. Other times, fabric prints require more thought into how you should cut them – on the grain, across the grain or at an angle? If you want a directional print to stay directional in your final quilt, now is the time to plan how to achieve that outcome.

Before you start cutting the fabrics you'd like to use, open them up and see how they read. Stand across the room and squint, take a digital photo and view it on your phone or camera, or – my favourite – take off your glasses. Now you can see if the fabric reads as one colour, as a light or dark, or if the print has some aspect that makes it stand out more than you had originally thought.

Cut a test strip of any medium-to-large prints that you plan to use. Once the medium print is cut into diamonds or hexagons, can you still see the print?

Do the flowers or people now look like blobs? Does the focus fabric print on a white background suddenly lose its sharpness against the solid white patches that it will be stitched to?

If the crisp lines of your EPP are lost because of misplaced prints, consider fussy cutting, or using those pattern curves to accentuate part of your design. Another option would be to swap the background fabric for something that has more contrast (for example, a solid instead of a tonal, or a dark rather than a light) or that won't compete with the larger motif fabrics.

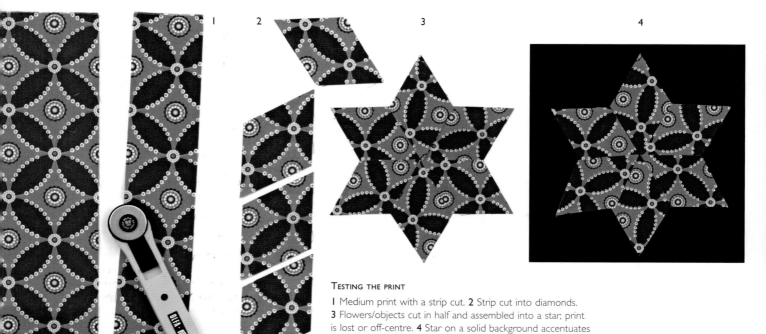

TESTING THE PRINT

1 Medium print with a strip cut. **2** Strip cut into diamonds.
3 Flowers/objects cut in half and assembled into a star; print is lost or off-centre. **4** Star on a solid background accentuates newly formed pattern.

Use the 'window' of a template to select an interesting part of the fabric pattern. Mark around the template and cut out.

Fussy cutting

Fussy cutting is when you centre a motif or repeat on your template so that it becomes the focal point of your EPP block. Various effects can be achieved by repeating the same fussy cut and then carefully arranging them when you stitch them together.

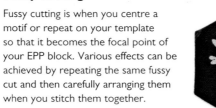

Using stripes

If you'd like to use stripes, how do you want them to appear when your pattern is put together? If you cut them from strips as you would a solid or all-over print, they will make your stars turn into swirls.

Cutting can make stripes a striking addition to EPP projects (see pattern on page 116). Put strips face to face before cutting out pairs, ensuring that the 'leaves' have diagonal lines that run together. Cutting on an angle can making your print read straight (see the Laptop Bag on page 84).

MIRRORED STRIPES
Cutting stripes in mirror images gives veins to 'leaves'.

STRIPES IN DIFFERENT DIRECTIONS
Cutting stripes from a strip makes them swirl around a star.

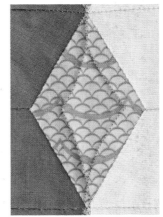

WORKING WITH DIRECTIONAL PRINTS
If you want directional prints to stay directional once pieced into the quilt, you may need to cut them on an angle to keep them straight and in order on your quilt top.

NEUTRAL BACKGROUND
The background fabric used here is an assortment of neutrals in similar shades. Some have text, some have a small print – but they all work well together and give depth and interest to the quilt.

Selecting a fabric colour palette

I love a scrappy, 'anything goes' quilt, but it still needs a unifying feature. The Travel Quilt on page 100 uses white stars and a red EPP border. When choosing that unifying feature, think outside of the box: your solid doesn't need to be white; try a range of neutrals or small prints/blenders. Your unifier doesn't need to be the centre of your puzzle pieces (for example, a star), or the background. Perhaps one template shape in a multi-template pattern will have the same fabric, or all of piece X will be white (see below). Just choose a feature and repeat it across the entire quilt top – that way no matter what else you add in, the quilt will look composed and well designed.

If you are having trouble finding a jumping point for your palette, find an inspirational photo – maybe a family snapshot or a catalogue advertisement. The internet is full of inspiration, but so are the print resources lying around your home.

Equally inspiring are clothing items and textiles that you see every day. Perhaps a scarf or necklace has just the right balance of colours that you could see yourself translating into a quilt. The Tanuki Stripe Throw (see page 92) was inspired by a floral blouse, which I managed not to cut up for fabric!

INSPIRED BY CLOTHING
The colours in this blouse inspired the palette for the Tanuki Stripe Throw on page 92.

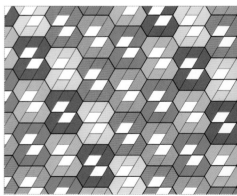

USING WHITE
In this variation of a half hexagon and diamond pattern, one diamond of each unit is kept white while the other fabrics could be any colour. This allows you to make that one template the unifying feature of your entire quilt top.

The good and the ugly

When you are choosing fabrics from your stash or scrap bin to cut for a project, don't just take all the pretty ones. The 'uglies' will never be used up if you keep passing them over – and who knows? When pieced in next to another block, the uglies might become cute. Here, an older floral print is joined by brighter fabrics to make a star that works.

Red-orange *Orange*

Red *Yellow-orange*

Red-violet *Yellow*

Violet *Yellow-green*

Blue-violet *Green*

Blue *Blue-green*

Stretch it out

If you are running out of a fabric, start interspersing your 'stretcher fabric' as early in the construction of the quilt top as you can. Even if only a quarter of the quilt has two greys in the background, it's more interesting than having just the bottom edge in a new fabric.

Your indispensable colour tool

Colours can be visualised in a circle or 'wheel'. There are numerous ways of dividing this wheel and using it to mix and match your fabrics.

- **Primary colours** are red, yellow and blue. They are pure colours – not made by mixing other colours – and are bold and bright.

- **Secondary colours** are orange, green and violet, made by mixing adjacent primary colours. Yellow and red make orange, yellow and blue make green, and blue and red make violet.

- **Tertiary colours** are made by mixing adjacent primary and secondary colours. For example, red (primary) and orange (secondary) will create red-orange. The tertiaries extend one colour into another.

- **Analogous colours** are any three adjacent colours on the wheel, such as blue, blue-violet and violet. These combinations have a calm, harmonious effect.

- **Complementary colours** are opposite each other on the wheel, such as blue and orange. They make each other appear more intense and vivid.

- **Triadic colours** are at the corners of an equilateral triangle overlaid on the wheel, such as red, yellow and blue or orange, green and violet.

- **Quadratic colours** are colours at the corners of a square or rectangle overlaid on the wheel, such as red-violet, orange, yellow-green and blue.

Making the most of scraps

For many quilters, the hobby comes with an ingrained sense that we must be frugal and not waste a single leftover bit of fabric. Some of us desire to save and use every scrap until it becomes an obsession. Often, the bin of scraps keeps growing but rarely gets used. Let's look at some ways you can pull those gems from the bottom of the pile and put them in a quilt, where they belong.

Scrap organisation

If I know I'm working on a scrappy EPP project, whenever I cut fabric for another quilt and have a scrap strip, I'll sub-cut it into the required EPP shape (for example, diamonds) and set the pieces aside on my cutting table or right into my sewing kit. EPP is a great 'on-the-side' project, and this habit stops you from having to sort fabric and cut hundreds of diamonds at one time.

When the time comes to use your scraps, be smart about it. Set a goal. Maybe you want a multicoloured scrap quilt or a monochrome scrap quilt. Perhaps you want to feature all of your favourite fabrics from one designer or to show off one fabric from each quilt you have made. It is easy just to reach into the bin and cut up whatever you pull out first, but a good scrap quilt needs balance. Follow the guidelines below to get yourself started on the right path.

- **Don't cut up an entire large scrap into your EPP shape without paying careful attention to how this will throw off the colour balance or distribution in your quilt top.** I don't mean that you should plan out each star from the beginning, but perhaps start by cutting up smaller scraps, or scraps of one colour, or one star's worth of scraps from one fabric, before slicing up your entire scrap stash into 60-degree diamonds.
- **Try pulling two fabrics from your scrap bin and seeing how they play together.** Pair a light and a dark and stitch one unit from them (for example, a 12-diamond star) and then use that as the structural element for the rest of your quilt. No matter what fabrics you add, so long as you stick to your light/dark combo, the quilt will read as a unified pattern.

- **Try using the wrong side of a fabric to add variety to your stash.** It can become a solid, appear more muted or give different shades to the dye (especially with batiks).
- **When cutting your EPP patches, don't worry about straight of grain.** On patches so small, with so many bias edges in the entire quilt, so long as you tack securely and don't distort the fabric as you do so, it really shouldn't matter.
- **Dealing with an unattractive scrap is part of the scrap-management process.** You have a few options – force yourself to cut it up and use it (maybe you could pair it with a fabric you love), or pass it on to someone else who might use it and love it. Holding on to a fabric you don't want to use is just distracting you from finding the scrap you were really looking for.

Storage and sorting scraps

Clear plastic containers or drawers in assorted sizes work very well for sorting scraps. While some quilters prefer to sort by colour, so that it's easy to see at a glance the various options available, I tend to sort by fabric size. That way, if I need a scrap of a certain size, I can just pull my 'small chunks' bin and know I can get three to four diamonds from any scrap in there. If I know I need six diamonds to make a star, I'll start in the strips bin, where I'm more likely to find a scrap that can accommodate my needs.

Preparing a travel tool kit

In order to make the most of your sewing time, and to let hand sewing fit into your busy life, you need to be prepared. The best way to go is to create your very own portable tool kit.

By having a secure place to keep your notions, fabric and templates, it is easy to grab your kit and go, tossing it into your bag on the way out the door to football practice, a doctor's appointment or a long bus or train ride. When piecing in public, the box can double as a work space on your lap, giving you a place to store your tools and stray threads. When you've got to stop and get up, it closes and latches securely so that you can slip it into your bag. Even if the contents get jumbled around inside the box, it's easier to sort them out than if you were searching the bottom of your bag for a thimble.

What to look for in a good case

Cases come in all shapes and sizes. Hard plastic, latching pencil cases are my favourites, but you can also use cosmetics pouches, tins, kids' lunch boxes or soft fabric bags. What is important is that your tools and fabric are secure inside, and that it is easy to open and shut to take advantage of the time you have to sew.

- **Clear plastic cases are great,** especially if you have several EPP projects going at one time. Then you can easily see which project is in which case, and which case contains your thimble!
- **Look for a case that closes securely** and doesn't have any openings where small tools, templates or paper clips could slide out.
- **Find a case that fits comfortably** into the bag that you use most often. If it is convenient, it is more likely you'll carry it with you and get more sewing done.

Decorative boxes may not make good travel sewing kits, but that doesn't mean you can't use them while you are piecing at home. I used to keep an EPP kit in the drawer of my coffee table and take it out to stitch while watching TV (or, more accurately, while my husband watched TV). When guests come over or your child wakes from a nap, it is easy to slip off your thimble and drop what you're doing. Close up the box and tuck it back into the drawer for an easy clean-up.

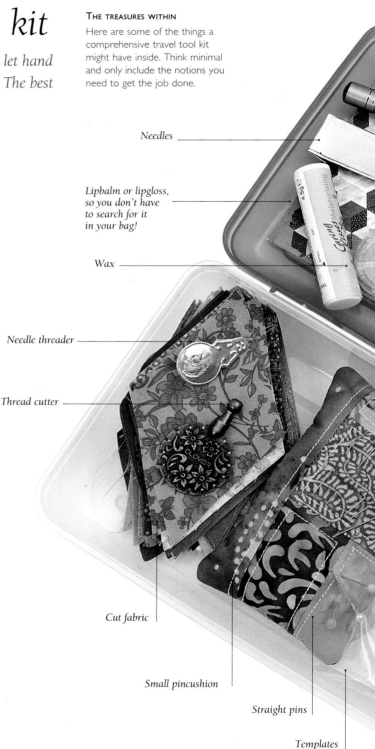

THE TREASURES WITHIN
Here are some of the things a comprehensive travel tool kit might have inside. Think minimal and only include the notions you need to get the job done.

Needles _____

Lipbalm or lipgloss, so you don't have to search for it in your bag! _____

Wax _____

Needle threader _____

Thread cutter _____

Cut fabric

Small pincushion

Straight pins

Templates

Paper clips

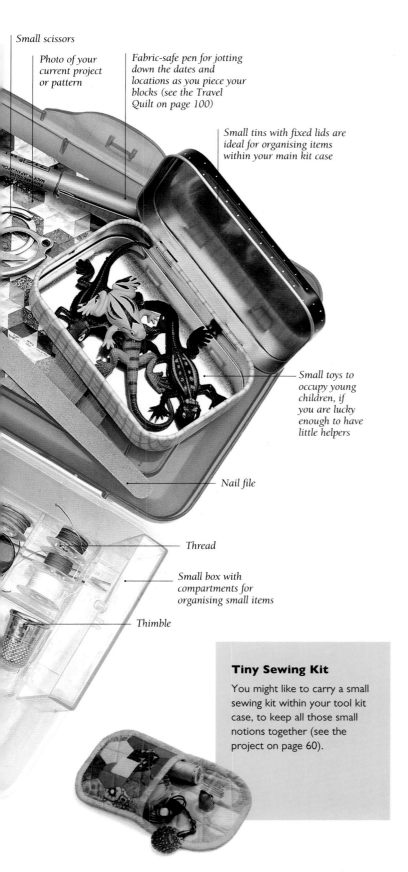

Small scissors

Photo of your current project or pattern

Fabric-safe pen for jotting down the dates and locations as you piece your blocks (see the Travel Quilt on page 100)

Small tins with fixed lids are ideal for organising items within your main kit case

Small toys to occupy young children, if you are lucky enough to have little helpers

Nail file

Thread

Small box with compartments for organising small items

Thimble

Tiny Sewing Kit

You might like to carry a small sewing kit within your tool kit case, to keep all those small notions together (see the project on page 60).

TIPS

- I usually keep a spool of thread for tacking and a spool of neutral thread for piecing. If my pattern calls for specific thread colours, I wind bobbins in the colours I need and tuck them into the small sewing kit, allowing me to save space and keep things organised.

- Use small zip-top bags to keep your templates and paper clips from sliding around inside the box.

- If you don't want to print out a photo of your current project, keep one on your phone or digital camera so that you can refer back to it as you piece away from home.

- When stitching near children, they are bound to get curious. Some safe ways to get them involved or let them 'help' include: passing you pairs of paper clips as you attach the fabric to the templates, letting them sort fabric colours or count out the number of shapes you need for your pattern, asking which colour or shape comes next in your sequence, or letting them choose the next fabric you'll stitch (great for scrappy patterns).

- While a small pair of scissors or a thread cutter is essential to your travel sewing kit, if you are planning to take your project on an airplane, it is best to check with the security organisation of the countries you will be travelling through, as travel security rules change frequently. I have never had any trouble taking my pendant thread cutter on a plane – domestic or international – but to be on the safe side, pack a small nail clipper or spool of dental floss separate from your sewing kit, in case your cutter doesn't make it through security. Never try to take scissors on board an airplane in your hand luggage.

Although putting together a quilting travel tool kit does take some prep work, once it's done you can quilt just about anywhere. I've done Hawaiian appliqué on the beach in Crete, pieced stars in the airport in Tokyo and quilted placemats during a road trip to Savannah.

Preparing the project

We have learned a lot about EPP so far and I'm sure you are itching to get started. Some people like to pick a shape and dive in, but remember that you will be spending a lot of time with this quilt, so it may be best to prepare a plan of action before you get carried away.

Templates

The templates used in EPP can be made from a variety of materials. The most popular are heavy paper, cardstock and flexible plastic.

The different materials all have their own benefits, and English paper piecers will all swear by their preferred types. Some shapes and patterns and construction methods work better with one type of template than another (for example, paper templates can be folded to sew a 'Y' seam), but some patterns can be made with any type. I tend to choose templates based on a few simple factors.

1 How big do I plan to make the quilt? (Plastic templates are by far my preferred option, but paper ones are considerably less expensive.)
2 What pattern am I going to try and what size templates do I want?
3 How portable do I need it to be? If I'm planning to make several puzzle pieces and join them later at home, I may be able to do it with one pack of templates, but if I already have half of the bed-sized quilt completed and joined at home, and I'm packing for a long holiday, I'll need two packs to keep going.

Try out as many template types as you can. The Resources on page 140 lists several online shops for purchasing templates.

Here are a few of the things I have discovered from working with templates:

• **Paper templates are good value.** They are less expensive than their plastic counterparts, but usually have a shorter lifespan. After tacking and piecing with them several times, the edges start to show wear and the points may not be as sharp. However, one of the undeniable benefits is that you can fold them, which allows for greater flexibility in the sequence in which you stitch the templates together. You can piece a long row of paper hexagons and then attach it to another long row quite easily, whereas with plastic, the templates don't bend enough for the pieces to lay flat

against each other as you stitch, and it is often necessary to stitch around all sides of a template and pop it out before going on to an intersecting seam.

• **Plastic templates are well worth the extra cost.** While it is true that they do not come in as many shapes or sizes as the paper variety, their durability is impressive. I have pieced three 60-degree diamond quilts with the same set of templates. Of course, the edges do get rough with pin pricks and start to show wear, but the corners don't lose their points and they never become flimsy from being bent. An additional benefit is that the thicker plastic templates also give an edge for the needle to glide along while whipstitching, and some quilters feel it is easier to piece this way.

• **There are plenty of quilters who swear by cutting their own templates,** and if you are interested in doing so, you can find information on where to print your own templates from the internet (see page 140). Templates for the projects in this book can be found on page 139 – you could photocopy and cut these out if desired. I much prefer the convenience of pre-cut templates and feel the time spent cutting my own would be better spent stitching.

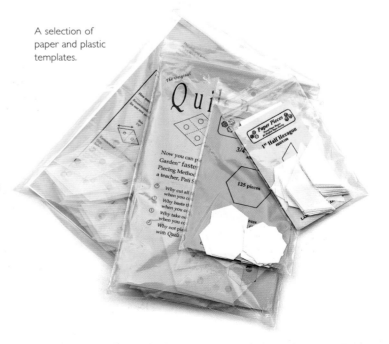

A selection of paper and plastic templates.

Graph paper

Graph paper is a useful tool when working out how you want your finished quilt to look. You can play around with colour schemes, block placement and spacing, and edges all before you cut a single piece of fabric.

This preliminary stage will also help you determine a size for your quilt and give you an idea of how much fabric you'll need. Refer to the cutting chart on page 37 to see how many pieces you can get from a strip cut from one width of fabric. Do the maths to see how much fabric you'll need for the entire quilt top.

There are ten types of graph paper at the end of this book, on pages 128–137. They coordinate with the ten patterns in the Patterns chapter (see pages 104–125). There are also some great online resources where you can download or print your own graph paper (see Resources on page 140).

Initial considerations

Take time to think about the following considerations and how you want to feature them in your project.

One-patch patterns

One-patch quilts are beautiful for their simplicity as well as their never-ending pattern possibilities. The humble hexagon can turn into a flower, diamond or ring, or give way to an impressive mosaic. Sixty-degree diamonds and half hexagons are two more shapes that have the potential to turn into stunning quilts without the help of any other shapes.

Combining shapes

Once you start playing with angles, it's tough not to want to see how far you can go. Many of the standard EPP template shapes combine nicely to make complex block patterns, which can be further enhanced by your placement of colours and fabrics. Check out the Patterns chapter on pages 104–125 for a few examples to get you started.

Dealing with the edges

When your general pattern has taken shape, give some thought as to how you will address the edges. There is more information on this in Chapter 2 (see Edges and Borders on page 46), but at the preparation stage it's a good idea to sketch out some possibilities so that you know how much fabric you will need and if you will need to purchase any additional template shapes (for example, half hexagons to fill in the edges of a hexagon quilt). For example, if you are working with a multi-shaped block, it may be necessary to stitch up half blocks or partial blocks to go along the edges. A pattern such as the rings of squares and triangles on page 124 does not naturally end in straight edges. Instead of purchasing half-shaped templates, in this case it may be more practical to piece partial blocks and cut them once you are ready to add borders.

Graph paper helps you to plan a quilt.

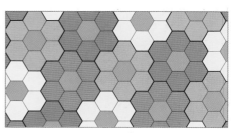

HEXAGONS

The hexagon is very versatile as a one-patch pattern.

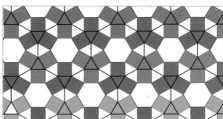

RINGS

Patterns that combine multiple shapes may require extra blocks to be made to fill in the edges of your quilt before you can attach borders.

chapter

2

Starting to sew

As well as familiarising yourself with the basics of English paper piecing, put a few tricks up your sleeve to make the work go faster. Have a bunch of ideas at your disposal for ways to finish your projects, so that you can enjoy the process — and the end result — as much as possible.

Cutting

Unlike other quilting methods, cutting in English paper piecing does not have to be precise. As long as you have enough seam allowance to tack around your template, there's no need to worry about accuracy. That said, it's a good idea to cut a generous seam allowance to allow some extra fabric to hold on to while tacking.

Cutting strips

1 Start with a length of fabric in front of you, no longer than your ruler, around 18in (46cm). If you are cutting from a full yard or metre, fold the fabric two or three times to make it more manageable.

2 Follow the chart on page 37 to determine the width of the strip you need. Cut one strip on your cutting mat, using a rotary cutter and acrylic quilter's ruler.

Tools & materials
Length of fabric
Cutting mat
Rotary cutter
Acrylic quilter's ruler
Specialist ruler

Working in threes

You can cut several strips and stack them – no more than three strips at a time – before sub-cutting your shapes. Remember that accuracy isn't necessary, so 'close enough' is good.

For diamonds

1 Turn your ruler and, using the 60-degree line on your cutting mat as a guide, trim off the edge of the strip.

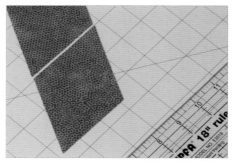

2 Rotate the strip on your cutting mat. Line up your width mark with the 60-degree line you just cut and sub-cut into diamonds.

Blunt diamonds

Diamonds don't need to have a sharp point. A blunt point will just leave less of a flag when tacked.

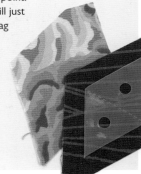

Cutting in batches

• I highly recommend NOT cutting all of the patches for your project at one time. By only cutting enough to fill your sewing kit, you can test out fabric combo ideas and substitute some if necessary. (Collect any cut rejects in a bin for a future scrap project such as the Travel Quilt, page 100.) Then you'll find a better balance and have something to do when you need a break from tacking and piecing. Your hands and fingers will appreciate a rest once in a while.

• If I know I need a lot of one colour, I'll cut 18in (46cm) x width of fabric and only cut that many patches at a time.

• By cutting in batches, you give yourself time to get back to your sewing table, restock your travel sewing kit, reassess your project, reflect, take 'in progress' photos or write a blog post about it.

Using scraps

When cutting from scraps, try to make the most of your fabric and don't pay attention to the straight of grain. English paper piecing patches are so small that, in the whole scheme of the quilt, the straight of grain really won't be noticed.

For triangles

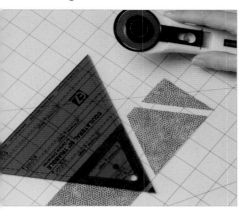

Cut strips with a specialist ruler, such as an equilateral triangle ruler, and leave a blunt tip on top of your fabric triangle.

For hexagons and squares

It is much faster to cut squares of fabric to tack around hexagons than to try to cut out individual hexagons. There is a bit of extra fabric folded over on the back, but the bulk isn't a problem, even when hand quilting (see Hexagon Cushion, page 64).

Fussy cutting

If you want to fussy cut your fabric to make kaleidoscope images or to highlight pictures on novelty-print fabrics, a special notion is available to help you (see page 25).

For half hexagons

1 Place your specialist ruler (here, an equilateral triangle ruler) over a template laid on the fabric. Estimate a comfortable seam allowance and cut.

2 Flip the ruler over and sub-cut.

Cutting chart

Shape	Length per side in inches (cm)		Width of strips to cut side in inches (cm)		Number of shapes that can be cut from width of fabric (assuming 42/107 usable inches/cm)
60° Diamonds	1	(2.5)	1½	(3.8)	24
	1¼	(3.2)	1¾	(4.4)	20
	1½	(3.8)	2⅛	(5.5)	17
	2	(5)	2⅝	(6.5)	12
Hexagons	¾	(1.9)	2	(5)	21
	1	(2.5)	2½	(6.4)	16
	1½	(3.8)	3½	(8.9)	12
	2	(5)	4½	(11.4)	9
Half hexagons	1	(2.5)	1½	(3.8)	17
	1½	(3.8)	2⅛	(5.5)	13
	2	(5)	2⅝	(6.5)	10
Triangles	1	(2.5)	1½	(3.8)	33
	1½	(3.8)	2⅛	(5.5)	25
	2	(5)	2½	(6.4)	21
	3	(7.6)	3¼	(8.3)	14
Squares	1	(2.5)	1¾	(4.4)	24
	1½	(3.8)	2¼	(5.7)	18
	2	(5)	2¾	(7)	15

Tacking

Every patch needs to be tacked, so with all that practice you'll be a pro in no time. Properly tacked pieces will result in better nesting of corners and a finished patchwork piece that lies flatter. By fanning out the seam allowances at acute angles, you can reduce bulk at the intersections and have a piece that is easier to quilt later.

Tools & materials

Templates made of paper, cardstock or flexible plastic

Cut fabric patches

Paper clips

Thread (cotton, polyester, blends or whatever you have on hand)

Needle

Thimble

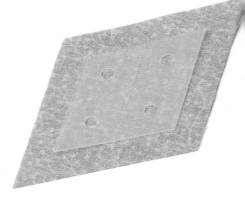

1 Place your template in the centre of the wrong side of your cut fabric. Here, a plastic template is used.

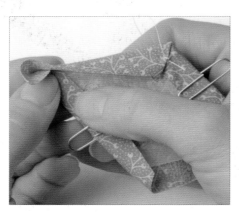

2 Fold over one edge of the seam allowance and hold it in place with a paper clip. Fold over the opposite edge, smoothing the fabric along the back of the template, and secure the second edge with another paper clip. Some shapes, such as hexagons or ones with sides longer than 2in (5cm), may need more than two paper clips. Do whatever you feel comfortable with.

3 Knot your thread and fold in your first edge, using your thumbnail to crease the fabric along the edge of the template as you make the fold. Take a backstitch through the fabric only – do not sew through the template.

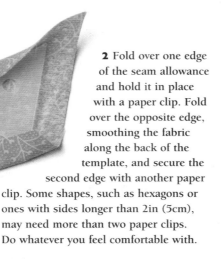

4 Fold in the next edge, again creasing and smoothing the fabric before you take another backstitch. You may find it helpful to use your thumbnail again to hold the fabric in place as you move the needle through.

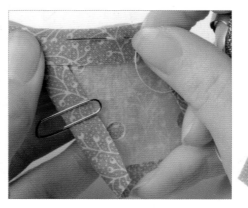

5 Fold over and secure all of the following corners in the same manner, removing the paper clips as you go. For pieces with sides 2in (5cm) or longer, catch the fabric once or twice between backstitches to keep it in place and taut along the template edge.

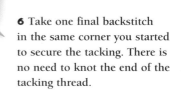

6 Take one final backstitch in the same corner you started to secure the tacking. There is no need to knot the end of the tacking thread.

Tacking stages of popular patches

1 Paper or plastic template laid in centre of wrong side of fabric

2 Paper clips attached

3 Taking the first backstitch

4 Completely tacked piece

SQUARE

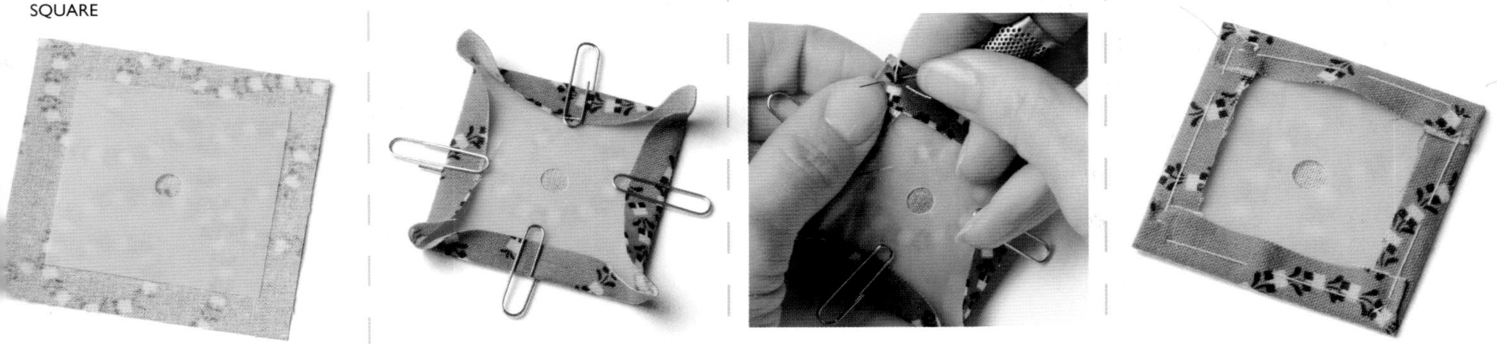

HEXAGON

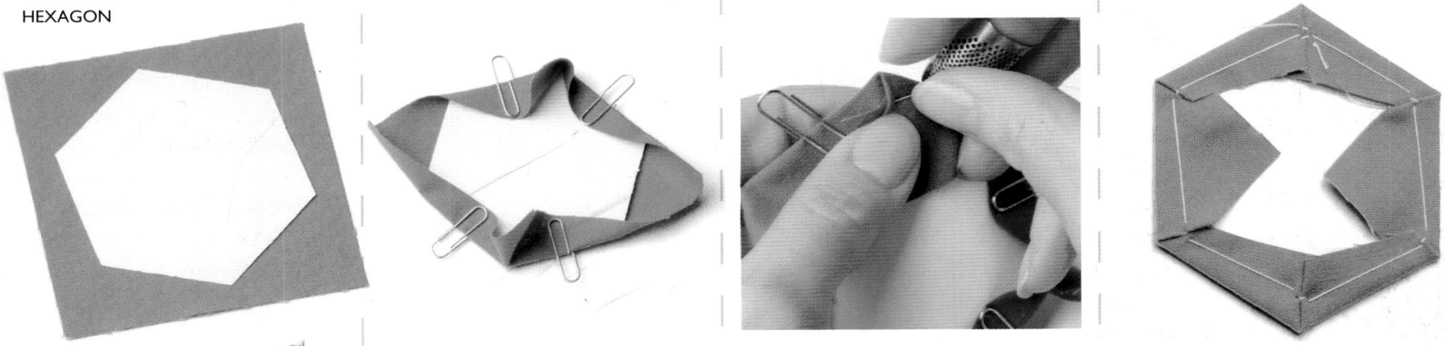

HALF HEXAGON

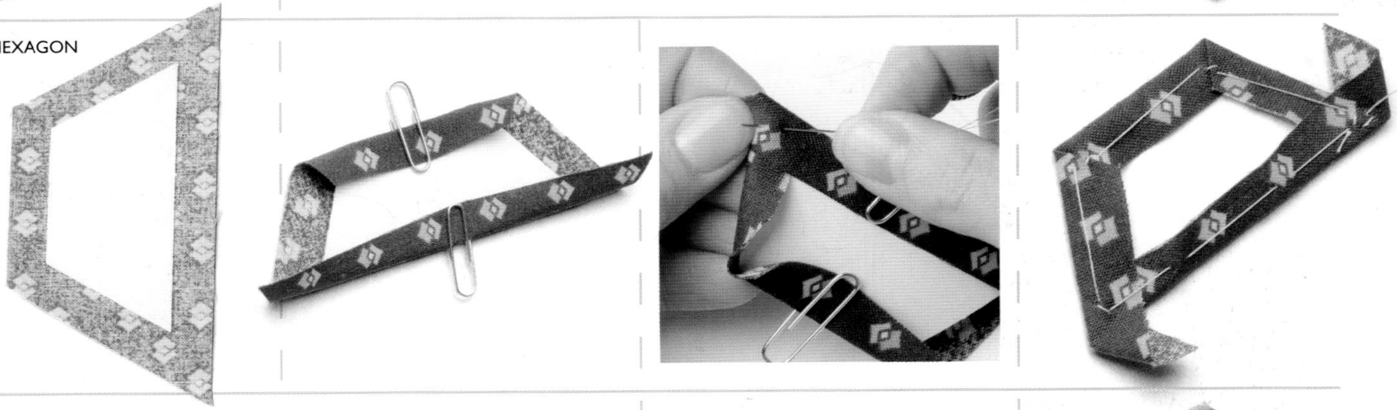

TRIANGLE

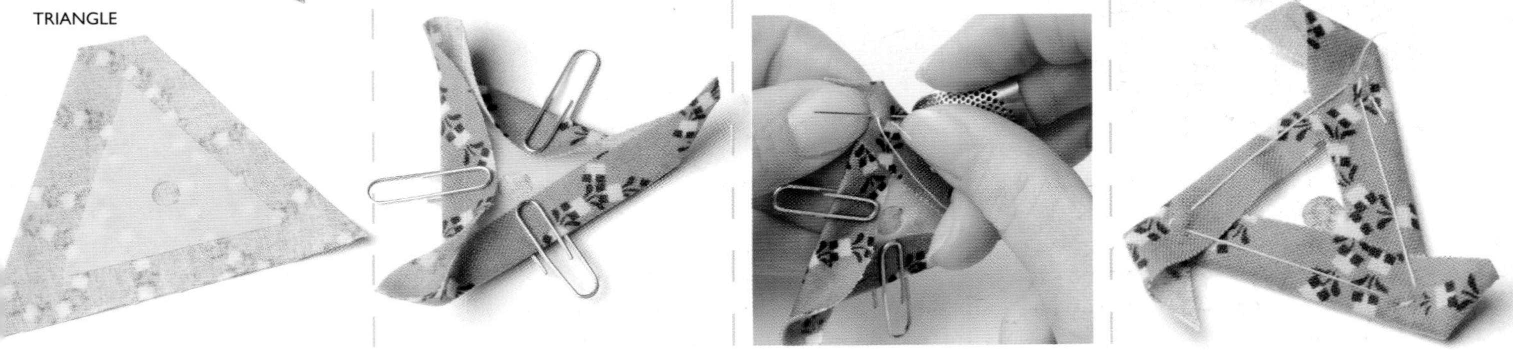

Whipstitching

Now that you've cut and tacked your fabric, you're ready to start sewing. There are a few different stitches that you can choose to sew together your templates in English paper piecing, but probably the most common is the whipstitch.

Tools & materials
Cotton thread
Needle
Thimble
Patch template

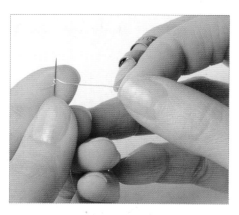

1 Start by knotting the end of a single strand of cotton thread, 12–18in (30–46cm) long.

2 Pick the corner you wish to start with and, from the back, work the needle from the seam allowance towards the corner with three small stitches to secure your knot in the fabric.

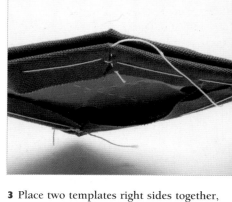

3 Place two templates right sides together, holding back any fabric tails from the area you are going to sew.

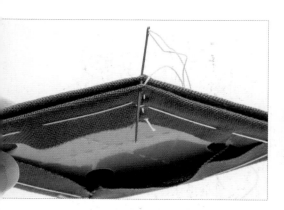

4 Take a stitch into the corner of the second template and back through the first, then pull securely.

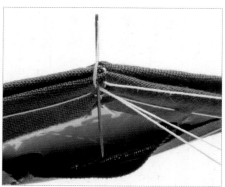

5 Take another stitch in the same spot, this time wrapping the thread around the needle before pulling it through to make a small knot at the corner (a 'wrap knot').

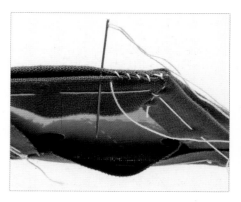

6 Begin to stitch from corner to corner, taking small bites of fabric along the edge of the template. Do not sew through the template material. Instead, use the template as a guide to slide the needle along as you take each stitch.

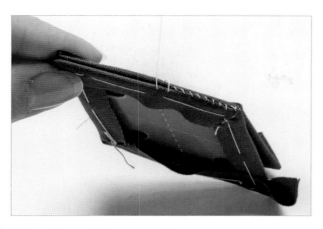

Spreading tension

As you are whipstitching, allow the thread to move through the eye of the needle so that tension is put on a different part of the thread every few stitches. This will avoid one point becoming too weak too quickly.

7 Every three stitches or so, pull your thread taut to tighten the stitches and make them 'melt' into the fabric.

8 When you reach the end of the template, take an extra stitch and slip the needle through the thread to knot it (wrap knot).

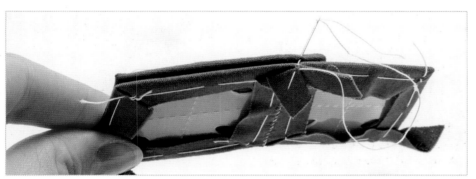

9 To join another template, leave the thread as it is, open the first two templates and place a new one along the seam you plan to sew. Take two stitches in the same spot of the corner and again make a wrap knot to secure it. Whipstitch as before.

10 To end a line of stitching or when you come to the end of your thread, secure with a wrap knot, then take three stitches back along the seam you have just sewn. Then work your needle three times through the seam allowance to bury the thread before cutting it.

11 All edges of a template must be stitched before the template can be removed.

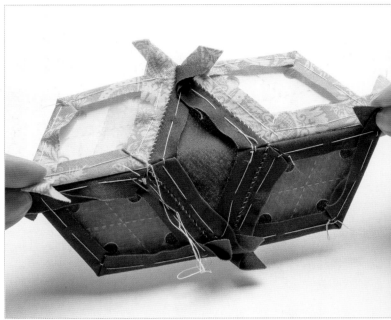

12 To remove a template, slide your finger or another pointed tool such as a small crochet hook inside the seam allowance and gently bend out the template. Plastic templates tend to 'pop', but paper templates may get wrinkled as you remove them. There is no need to cut the tacking thread or remove tacking stitches.

13 Depending on the type of template material you are working with, you may need to adjust the order of the seams sewn in order to pop out a centre template and be able to fold the piece to sew 'Y' seams. With plastic templates this is necessary, whereas paper templates can be folded.

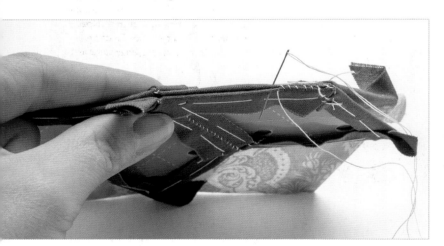

14 To join two pieced sections, start at one corner and stitch as above, making a wrap knot at the start and end of each template piece.

15 Pay special attention to where several templates meet and be sure to reach in to pull up the edges of each fabric and stitch them tightly, thus avoiding any holes in between joined pieces.

16 The sample star uses white thread and dark fabric to show that, with whipstitching, some thread will be visible on the front side of the patchwork. For this reason, it is best to piece with a neutral or matching thread colour.

Knotted thread

If your thread gets tangled and knotted as you are sewing, stick your needle in the loop and pull until the loop closes. Then grasp both ends of the thread near the knot and pull. The knot should pop itself out. If it doesn't, cut the thread and start over.

Weak spot in the thread

Repeated friction against the eye of the needle can wear down cotton thread, so if you find a weak spot while stitching, take a few backstitches and then work the thread into the seam allowance to hide the weak spot. Bring the needle up again where you left off, make a wrap knot and continue stitching.

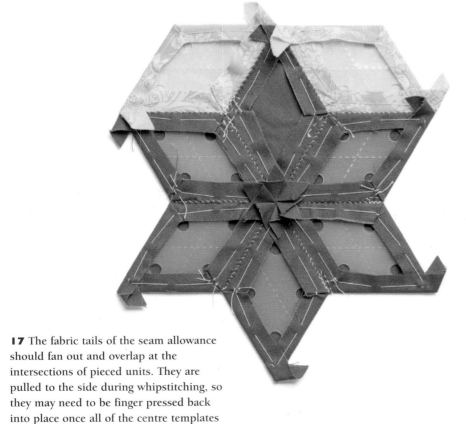

17 The fabric tails of the seam allowance should fan out and overlap at the intersections of pieced units. They are pulled to the side during whipstitching, so they may need to be finger pressed back into place once all of the centre templates have been removed.

Broken thread

If there is enough of a tail left, try to rethread the needle, make a wrap knot, backstitch and bury the thread tail. If not, just reknot the thread, start a few stitches back, bury the thread again and begin to sew over the last three to four stitches you made before the break. Make one or two wrap knots at the spot to ensure it is secure, then continue stitching.

Joining puzzle pieces

By unlocking the puzzle of the pattern, you will find piecing becomes a game and progresses surprisingly quickly. Soon your travel tool kit (see page 30) will be full of pieced units and it will be time to let your quilt start to take shape.

Tools & materials
Needle
Thread
Thimble

Trying out combinations

Once you've made a bunch of pieces, it's time to start playing around to see how they are going to come together in your final quilt.

See how the fabrics work together. Rearrange as many times as you like, or trust your gut instinct.

It helps to step back or take a digital photo of your layout to see how the colours play together. Sometimes simple changes can affect the entire balance of the quilt. The example above left shows a bad balance, with three yellowish stars next to each other. The example above right shows a good balance.

See if the pieces would look better with fillers in between or joined right next to each other. Play around with different filler fabrics before cutting into them.

If you have made all of the puzzle pieces uniform (in colour distribution or orientation), they may create secondary patterns when they are joined. If this is your plan, take care in how you join them.

Joining groups

When you've got eight or ten units joined, stop and do another batch of the same. Then join the two larger bits. Don't join one unit to the whole at a time – this puts too much strain on the seams already stitched and the whole piece is manipulated more than necessary.

At some point soon, you'll need to join your sections in order to free up some templates so that you can refill your travel sewing kit. Fit two larger sections together, adding in extra units if necessary to balance out your colours.

Building out the edge

Once you've got a good base (10–20 units), build out an edge. Continue joining smaller sections and then adding them to the whole until the quilt is the desired size. As the quilt grows, the templates in the edges (especially plastic ones) will start to weigh it down and put stress on those seams as you manipulate the top to join the final sections. If you have already chosen your edge technique (see pages 46–49), you may be able to remove edge templates and then press and tack the outer edges. This will not only free up templates, but will also reduce weight and strain on your quilt top. Take care not to remove any templates on portions to which you plan to join more units.

The end result

Whether you choose a planned-out layout or just let inspiration strike and add in random solid or differently coloured blocks here and there, your English paper-pieced project will be truly your own.

First join puzzle pieces into groups, then join the groups together to free up template pieces.

Handy reference tool

Sometimes I take a picture of the finished section so that I can refer to it as I join units in a new section, thus avoiding having any of the same fabrics or too many similar units next to each other. That way I can also see which colours are dominant or lacking in a certain area, and piece accordingly.

In the example below, the bottom edge is filled out with hexagons. More options for the edges can be found on pages 46–49.

Edges and borders

Once you've pieced the bulk of your units together, it's time to consider some border options. Here are some ideas that you can use, individually or in combination, to give your quilt the frame it needs.

Edges

EPP is full of wonderful angles, but these shapes and puzzle pieces don't always lend themselves to straight quilt edges. The beautiful units you've pieced may need a little more added on to turn them into an actual quilt top. Depending on the shapes used in your pattern, there are several options that you can choose for the edges of your quilt.

You can incorporate other shapes to take your EPP all the way to the edge of the quilt top, as shown above, or appliqué it on to border fabric to straighten the edge.

Option 1: Adding the same shape

You may be able to use the same template shape to fill out your edge.

A pattern of diamond stars can be smoothed by adding additional diamonds between the units along two edges. This technique makes a jagged edge, but the dips are more uniform and it will be easier to appliqué the quilt top to a border fabric or to cut the edges straight.

You can also add extra templates from your puzzle piece to fill in tiny gaps. This leaves a jagged edge, but makes it possible to add a 'border' with colour that can be used for contrast against a border fabric or the binding of the quilt.

Option 2: Adding a partial block

Depending on the shapes and angles used, you may be able to use a complementary shape, half shape or partial block to make a smoother edge.

You can use the same shapes from your puzzle piece to make up a half block. Here, half hexagons are used to make triangles, which smooth out this edge.

Use different shapes that have the same angles to smooth out the edge of your pattern. Here, hexagons are used to fill in the edge of a diamond star pattern.

Use half shapes (half hexagons for a hexagon pattern or triangles for a diamond pattern) to fill in gaps and make a completely smooth edge.

Borders

Once you've decided how to treat the edge of your EPP portion, the next step is to decide on the border. You could have a single border, a double border or a mitred border. You could also leave a straight edge.

Option 1: Single fabric border

The easiest way to get a straight edge on your angled EPP top is to add a single fabric border. This can be achieved in a variety of ways – see Appliqué Methods, opposite.

Option 2: Alternative methods

You can choose not to use a fabric border at all, and instead leave the edge of your quilt jagged, build out the edge with more EPP templates or use your rotary cutter and acrylic quilter's ruler to cut a straight edge, as done on the Rose Star quilt above.

Option 3: Multiple fabric borders

There is room for lots of colour play if you decide to add more than one fabric border. The EPP top can be appliquéd to the inner border first and then additional borders added, or you can stitch the borders together first, mitre them and then attach the EPP to them. (See the Travel Quilt on page 100.)

Option 4: For small projects

If your EPP project is small, you may be able to lay the EPP portion on to a solid piece of border fabric, appliqué it down and then cut away the excess fabric from the back. This way you do not need to piece individual border strips on to the four sides of the quilt. (See the Falling Stars Baby Quilt on page 88.)

Seam allowances

Keep in mind that your border fabric must be wide enough to go securely under the innermost points of your EPP pattern – with some designs, this means that a lot of fabric will be under some portions in order for a ½in (1cm) seam allowance to be under the narrow bits.

Appliqué methods

If you have chosen to add a border to your EPP quilt, you must choose a method with which to attach it. Most of the projects in this book use a machine topstitch to secure the EPP top to the fabric border, the edge of which has been tucked underneath to give an adequate seam allowance. If your EPP pattern has seam tails from when the fabric was tacked on to the template, be sure to tuck them under the completed top and press them into place securely, so that they don't pop out as you appliqué. You can also use one of the stitches on your sewing machine to appliqué the EPP top to the border. A blanket stitch may work, but avoid a zigzag stitch because it may distort your border fabric and become too bulky.

Seam tail

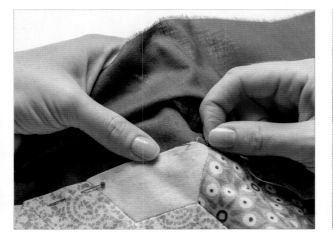

Option 1: Hand appliqué

To appliqué the EPP top down by hand, remove the edge templates, then press and tack the edge flat. Lay the EPP top on top of the border fabric, making sure that ½in (1cm) of border is tucked beneath the edge of the EPP top. Pin it in place, and attach with whipstitch (see page 40).

Option 2: Machine appliqué

Topstitching the EPP top to your border fabric is the most secure method of appliqué. First remove the edge templates, then press and tack the edge flat. Position the EPP top on top of your border fabric, making sure that you have a ½in (1cm) seam allowance. Pin the EPP top in place and stitch it down by machine, using a straight stitch and catching only ⅛in (3mm) or less of the edge as you go. Don't let the weight of the EPP portion distort your stitching line as you add the borders. Step-by-step instructions for topstitch appliqué can be found in the instructions for the Travel Quilt on page 100.

Assembling and finishing

On the following pages, you will find general guidelines and instructions for putting your entire quilt together. These tips and instructions will work for any other quilt you are making, as well as for EPP tops. As with everything in the craft of quilt making, there are many ways to get the job done. If your method differs from this guide, please do whatever works best for you.

Pressing

Before quilting your top on your home machine or sending it to a long-arm quilter, you must press the finished patchwork carefully,

- A good press ensures that the quilt top is flat and does not have any creases. It also flattens the quilt out to its actual size.
- As you press, make sure that the seams fall in the direction you had planned.

- Take time during this step to remove any stray threads or fuzz from your quilt top, especially on the underside – you don't want an errant dark thread peeking through your beautifully pieced white quilt top.

Backing fabric

The underside of the quilt is usually made from a single piece of fabric that is wider than the quilt top.

- Extra-wide backing fabric (108–120in [275–300cm]) is available from some fabric shops and many online retailers.
- You can piece your backing from standard-width fabric or an assortment of large pieces of fabric. Be sure to remove selvedges from the stitched edges and piece your backing with a ½in (1cm) seam allowance. Pieced backings have become quite popular as an added design element to quilts, and many great examples can be found on blogs and photo-sharing sites such as Flickr or Pinterest.
- If you are going to be sending your quilt out to a long-arm quilter, be sure to check with them about how to prepare your quilt top and how large the wadding and backing need to be in relation to the size of the quilt.

1 Start by laying your backing fabric face down on a wide, flat surface. Depending on the size of your quilt top, you may be able to do this on a large table or on the floor.

2 Using masking tape, tape your backing fabric to the floor or table at the edges. Start with the top and bottom centre, then do the sides and then the corners. Make sure that the fabric is taut but not distorted. Continue to tape around the edges until the backing is secure.

Wadding

There are many options for wadding, but whichever type you choose, a low-loft wadding works best for hand or machine quilting. Purchase a piece of wadding that is roughly 4in (10cm) bigger than your quilt top on all sides, and keep in mind that most waddings will shrink once the quilt is washed. Many quilters like the soft and wrinkled effect this gives, but if you would like to avoid it, wadding can be pre-washed. Refer to the manufacturer's instructions.

Get some help

Layering and tacking your quilt can be backbreaking work. Why not invite a friend to help you out? A second set of eyes can help make sure your layers are straight, and a second pair of hands will make the job go faster.

ADDED INTEREST
A pieced backing can give an additional layer of interest to your quilt.

3 Lay your wadding on top of your backing and carefully spread it out, being sure to flatten any wrinkles. You should be able to see 1in (2.5cm) of backing fabric all around the edge. Tape it down in a few places to hold it securely.

4 Lay your quilt top on top, right side up. Leave 2–4in (5–10cm) of wadding all around the edges. Smooth the quilt top out with your hands and tape it in place at the edges, in the same way that you taped down the backing, taping opposite edges to ensure that it is taut but not distorted. Assembling the three layers of the quilt – backing, wadding and quilt top – is known as making a 'quilt sandwich'.

Tacking

Quilts can be tacked in three ways: with temporary spray adhesive, with thread or with curved quilter's safety pins. The method you choose will be determined by the size of your project, how you plan to quilt it and your personal preference.

- **Spray adhesive** works well for smaller projects, such as the Small Pouch (see page 80) and Laptop Bag (see page 84).
- **Tacking thread** is a popular option if you plan on hand quilting, since the quilt can then easily be manipulated and moved around in a large or small quilting frame or hoop.
- **Pinning** is fast and effective, and very convenient if you plan to quilt by machine. This is the method we will use here.

Warning!

Tacking with safety pins may scratch or damage the floor or tabletop where you have laid out your project. It is best to find a suitable surface on which to tack, such as laminate tile or an area that you won't mind scratching.

5 Starting in the centre of your quilt, insert safety pins, being careful to collect all three layers before you bring the pin up again.

6 Place your pins 5–6in (13–15cm) apart across the top of your quilt, working in quadrants. There are specialist tools sold at quilting and fabric shops that can assist in closing the pins and saving your fingernails. If you can't find one, a spoon should do the trick.

7 Place a few extra pins all along the outer edge of your quilt top to keep it securely tacked.

Whether you choose to tack with thread or pins, be sure to tack the three layers securely to avoid them shifting as you quilt, which can result in puckers on your finished quilt.

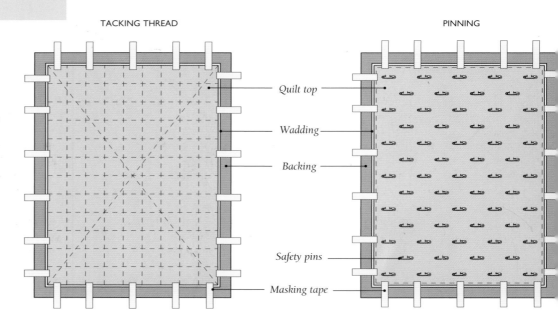

TACKING THREAD

PINNING

Quilt top

Wadding

Backing

Safety pins

Masking tape

Quilting (hand and machine)

Quilting adds beauty, stability and strength to your project. Whether you choose to quilt by hand or machine, your lines of quilting stitches should be no farther apart than 4–5in (10–13cm). There are many great print and online resources on both quilting methods.

8 Quilt your quilt as desired (see the options below).

9 If you have tacked the layers using thread, now is the time to remove the tacking stitches. If you have pinned the layers, you will have removed the pins as you quilted each section. When the quilting is finished, give the top a careful look over to be sure that no remaining tacking thread or pins are left.

10 Once your quilt is quilted, carefully trim away the excess wadding and backing fabric with your acrylic ruler, rotary cutter and cutting mat. You may want to use a large square ruler to ensure that each corner is 90 degrees.

Option 1: Domestic machine quilting
Machine quilting produces a distinct line and is regarded as a technique in its own right. Your quilt can be sewn in two ways – with a walking foot or in free-motion using a darning or embroidery foot.

Option 2: Long-arm quilting
Long-arm machine quilting services have become popular over the last few years. Most quilters don't have space for the large quilting frame at home, but you can send your quilt to a professional quilter if you don't want to do it yourself.

Option 3: Hand quilting
Quilting by hand can be done with the quilt in a hoop, on a frame or in your lap. Issues such as portability will affect your choice of method – lap quilting can be taken almost anywhere, while a frame will restrict you to quilting in one room.

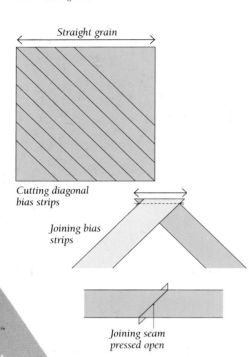

Straight grain

*Cutting diagonal
bias strips*

*Joining bias
strips*

*Joining seam
pressed open*

Bias binding

To cover the edges of the quilt, you will
need to make double-fold bias binding.
To find out how much binding you
will need, measure the four sides of
your quilt, add them together and
then add 12in (30cm).

1 Begin by cutting strips 2¼in (5.5cm) wide
on the 45-degree angle of your fabric. Join
the strips on the diagonal with a ¼in
(6mm) seam and trim the excess fabric.
Fold the strip in half lengthways and press,
wrapping the bias tape around a small
board or other handy tool to stop it from
getting tangled.

2 When you are ready to attach the
binding, first open the edge and fold
in about ¼in (6mm) of fabric. Press.

3 Start about 8–10in
(20–25cm) down from one
corner of your quilt and pin
the raw edge of the binding
to the front of your quilt,
aligning the edges.

4 Continue pinning until you
come to a corner. Insert a pin
through the binding and your
quilt at a 45-degree angle,
towards the corner of the quilt.
Then pull the binding up and
fold it at that angle before
folding it down on itself
and along the next edge
of the quilt.

5 Continue pinning the binding
along the edges of the quilt,
repeating step 4 at every corner.

6 When you reach your starting point, overlap the binding by about 1½in (4cm). Then open the binding strip and cut it at a 45-degree angle.

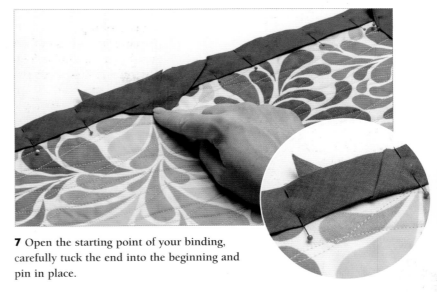

7 Open the starting point of your binding, carefully tuck the end into the beginning and pin in place.

8 Machine stitch the binding on with a ¼in (6mm) seam.

9 When you come to each corner, fold the flap out of the way and stitch to within ¼in (6mm) of the edge. Backstitch here to secure the corner. Then release the presser foot and, without cutting the threads, turn your quilt so that you are ready to sew the next side. Fold the binding flap back into place and stitch over it as you come down the new side, backstitching at the start to secure your corner point. When you come to the end of your binding, backstitch again to secure the threads before cutting them.

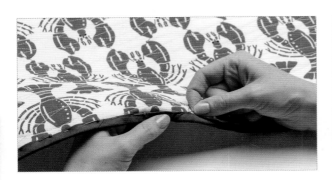

10 Fold the binding around to the back of your quilt and secure it with 5–6 straight pins. The binding fabric should cover the stitching line from step 8. Begin whipstitching the binding to the backing of your quilt, taking care not to let any stitches show on the front.

11 At the corners, fold the binding in along one side, creating a 45-degree angle at the edge. Then fold it back on to itself along the next side, creating a mitred look. Secure the corner with a few backstitches as you continue to whipstitch around the edge.

Labels

Quilts are a part of our material culture and have the possibility of becoming family heirlooms or being bought and sold as pieces of art. As a result, it is very important that you attach a label to each quilt you make. Labels can document who made the quilt, who it was made for, where it was made and if it came from a published pattern or from the quilter's own design.

1 To make a quilt label, you will need a light-coloured fabric, a piece of freezer paper (with a plastic coating on one side) and a fabric-safe pen or marker.

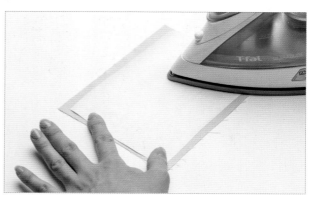

2 Begin by ironing the coated side of the freezer paper to the wrong side of your label. This will stabilise the fabric so that you can write on it.

3 Document your quilt's information with a fabric-safe pen. Consider including: the name of the quilt, your name, when and where it was made, who it was made for, your inspiration, information about the fabrics and care instructions (particularly if it is a gift).

4 Add any additional decorations you'd like, such as rubber-stamped images with fabric-safe permanent ink. Remove the freezer paper and press the label from the wrong side to heat-set the ink.

5 Fold in ¼in (6mm) on all sides and press the seams. Pin the label in place on the back of your quilt and attach it with whipstitch.

Tanuki Stripe
Made for
Amy & Jake
♥ with love ♥
by Jessica Alexandrakis
Westbury, NY

Falling Stars
designed by:
Jessica Alexandrakis
pieced with help from:
Becky Lovasz
Merrill Rosenberg
Bernadette Forward
Westbury, NY
quilted by:
Shannon Couvillion

Lesly Wader-Wooll
14 Johnson Stre
CANADA

Travel Quilt #3
2010 - 2012
designed & pieced by
Jessica Alexandrakis
Westbury, NY
quilted by Shannon Couvillion

3

The projects

Ready to try it out for yourself? This chapter features ten projects for you to practise your English paper-piecing skills. They range in difficulty and time intensity: the pincushion can be finished in a weekend, but you'll carry the larger quilts with you for a while. Before you know it, your home will be full of handmade goodness.

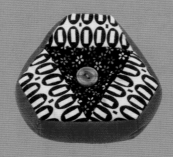

Quilting on the go is so much easier if you know that all your essential notions are safe and in one place. Whip up this tiny sewing kit and add it to your travel sewing kit to keep track of your needles, thimble, thread cutter and wax. When I take it out of my sewing box, I slip the needles next to the pins on the inner flap. It is lightweight and perfect for other hand-stitching projects as well, such as finishing binding or Hawaiian appliqué.

Tiny sewing kit

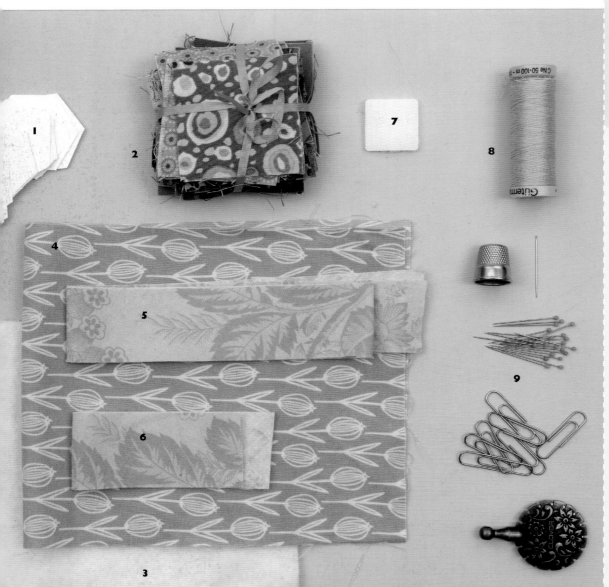

For templates, see pages 138–139

¾in (2cm)
Hexagon x 36

Sewing kit x 1

Dimensions

The EPP top measures approximately 4¼ x 11in (11 x 28cm) before assembly.

Tools & materials

36 x ¾in (2cm) hexagon templates **1**

36 x assorted 2in (5cm) fabric squares **2**

5 x 12½in (12.5 x 32cm) piece of wadding **3**

5½ x 13in (14 x 33cm) piece of lining fabric **4**

Two strips of bias binding:
22 x 1¼in (56 x 3cm) **5**
6 x 1¼in (15 x 3cm) **6**

Velcro dots **7**

Thread **8**

Sewing kit (thimble, needle, straight pins, paper clips, thread cutter) **9**

1 Tack your hexagons to the templates and stitch them in an arrangement that is pleasing to you, in four rows of nine. The final top should measure slightly larger than 4¼ x 11 in (11 x 28cm).

2 Remove the templates from the fabric hexagons and give the top a good press with a hot iron.

3 Layer, tack and quilt the EPP top (see Assembling and finishing, page 50).

4 Trace the project template on page 138 on to paper and cut it out. Choose which end of your quilt will be the body of the sewing kit and which will be the pocket flap. Lay the paper template on top of the quilt sandwich and, using a fabric pen, trace the template on to the quilted piece.

5 Remove the paper and cut out the pattern.

6 Use the smaller piece of bias binding to bind the straight edge of the pocket flap (see page 54 for instructions on binding).

Added security

If you prefer, you can pin your paper project template on to your quilt sandwich. This should make it more secure and therefore easier to trace around the template on to your fabric.

Pocket flap   *Body of sewing kit*

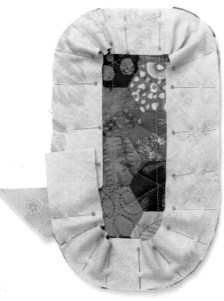

7 Fold the quilt sandwich as indicated on the template, and then pin the larger piece of bias binding to the outside edge. Gather and ease evenly around the corners, pinning between each gather (see pages 54–55 for instructions on starting and stopping binding).

8 Once you have pinned the bias binding all the way around the outside edge, it will be ready to sew in place.

9 Machine stitch the binding to the quilt top (see page 54).

10 Fold the binding over the raw edge of the quilt layers, turn the raw edge under itself and then pin in place. (The bias cut of the binding will allow you to stretch it around the corner.) Hand stitch in place, using whipstitch.

11 Mark the position of the Velcro closure and attach it by hand.

Hand and machine quilting

This project can be completed by hand or machine quilting, and hand or machine finishing. If you choose to hand quilt and attach the binding without a machine, use backstitch and be mindful of the hand-pieced threads you cut to get the sewing kit into the proper shape. Machine stitching the binding may be a better choice to ensure that no threads unravel.

Sometimes it's hard to find an accent piece that coordinates perfectly with your room. By adding a mix of fabrics to this cushion cover, you can pull together several elements in a room to solidify your personal style. The pattern also works well with fabric charm packs and layer cakes, or you could try swapping special fabrics or signature blocks with friends. The 1½in (4cm) per side hexagons stitch up quickly, giving you time to splurge on big-stitch hand quilting to make a soft and inviting addition to any sofa.

Hexagon cushion

For template, see page 139

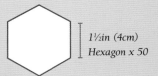

1½in (4cm)
Hexagon x 50

Dimensions

The finished cushion cover measures 16½ x 16½in (42 x 42cm).

Tools & materials

50 x 1½in (4cm) paper hexagon templates **1**

56 x 3½in (9cm) squares of fabric (use at least 14 different fabrics for good variety) **2**

20in (50cm) square piece of wadding **3**

20in (50cm) square piece of lining fabric **4**

Two pieces of fabric for the cushion back (top: 16½ x 8½in/42 x 22cm and bottom: 16½ x 12in/42 x 30cm) **5**

Button **6**

Hair elastic **7**

Temporary spray adhesive **8**

75in (1.9m) of bias binding, 2¼in (5.5cm) wide **9**

Thread for piecing, perlé cotton for hand quilting **10**

Sewing kit (scissors, paper clips, needle threader, needles, straight pins, thimble) **11**

16in (40cm) square cushion pad

1 Cut the fabric and tack to the templates (see pages 36–39).

2 Join them in eight rows of seven hexagons each, centring novelty prints. Remember that prints along the edge will be cut off when the cushion top is squared up. Remove the templates and give the top a good press.

3 Layer and tack with spray adhesive. The lining fabric can be calico or any fabric you are trying to use up.

4 Quilt with perlé cotton.

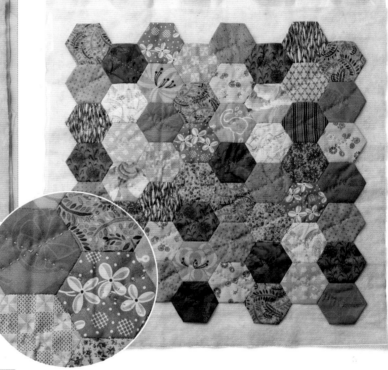

5 Using a square ruler, trim to 16 ½in (42cm) square.

6 Hem one long edge of each piece for the cushion back: first fold over ¼in (6mm) of one long edge and press with a hot iron, then fold over ½in (1cm) and press again before topstitching by machine.

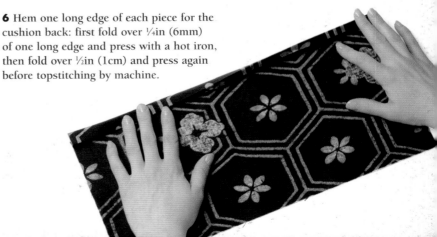

7 Place the two back pieces right sides up on the wrong side of the cushion front, with the hemmed edges in the centre, and mark where the button and elastic will go.

8 Attach the button by hand to the lower back piece and the elastic (right) by machine to the top back piece.

9 Place the two back pieces on the cushion top, wrong sides together, and pin in place. Pin the binding to the front of the cushion top. Attach the binding by machine, assembling the cushion back at the same time. Take care to backstitch at the openings of the cushion back.

10 Remove the pins, fold the binding to the cushion back and whipstitch by hand (see page 55). Stuff with a cushion pad and enjoy!

You can never have too many pincushions! This pattern incorporates four different-shaped templates for a unique-looking style. Crushed walnut shells, found at some quilt shops and most pet shops, are used as filling to give the cushion a nice weight. Keep one next to your machine to collect straight pins as you sew, and another on your cutting table to use as a weight to hold larger pieces of fabric in place as you measure and cut.

Pincushion

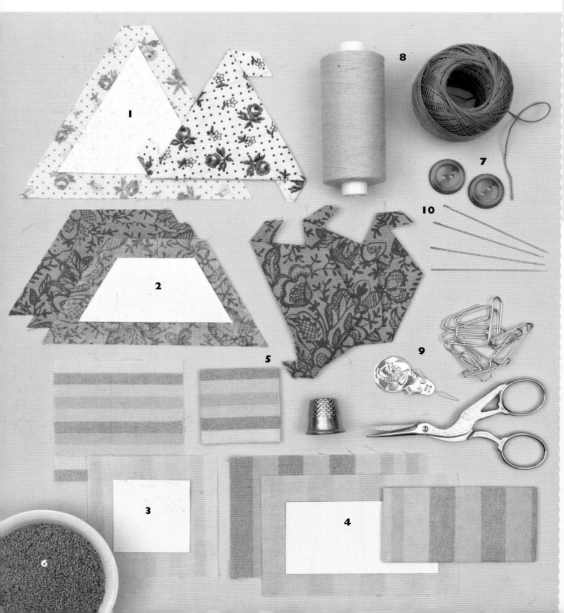

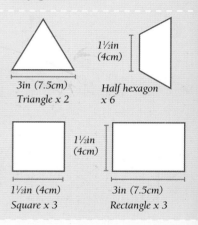

For templates, see page 139

3in (7.5cm)
Triangle x 2

1½in (4cm)
Half hexagon x 6

1½in (4cm)
1½in (4cm)
Square x 3

1½in (4cm)
3in (7.5cm)
Rectangle x 3

Dimensions

The pincushion measures 4½ x 4 x 1½in (12 x 10 x 4cm) at the widest points.

Tools & materials

2 x 3in (7.5cm) triangle templates **1**

6 x 1½in (4cm) half hexagon templates **2**

3 x 1½in (4cm) square templates **3**

3 x 1½ x 3in (4 x 7.5cm) rectangle templates **4**

Small pieces or scraps of three different fabrics **5**

Crushed walnut shells **6**

Two buttons **7**

Thread for piecing, thicker thread for attaching the buttons **8**

Sewing kit (thimble, needle threader, paper clips, scissors) **9**

Long needle for attaching the buttons **10**

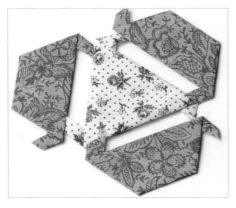

1 Cut the fabrics and tack to the templates (see pages 36–39).

2 Attach three half hexagons to each triangle.

3 Attach three squares and three rectangles to one of the triangle/half hexagon units.

4 Stitch the sides of the squares and rectangles together from the wrong side, leaving one square unsewn.

5 Remove the templates as you go.

6 Begin stitching the other triangle/half hexagon unit on to the sides, with the entire piece inside out.

7 When you reach the last square, finger press any remaining unsewn edges and take out all templates except for that square.

8 Turn the piece right side out.

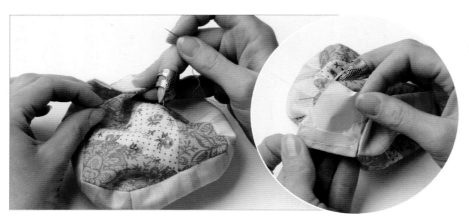

9 Sew half of the bottom edge of the unsewn square and take out the template (right).

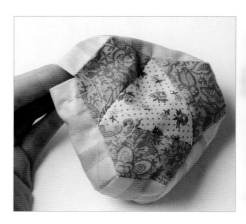

10 Stick your finger into the hole to help manipulate the fabric and keep the edge straight as you finish stitching the rest of the bottom-edge seam.

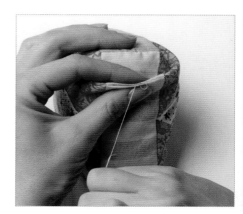

11 Using a funnel, add the crushed walnut shells until the pincushion is the desired thickness.

12 Stitch the opening closed using whipstitch.

13 Using a thicker thread, stitch buttons in the centre of the pincushion at the top and bottom, pulling the thread taut. After four loops through both buttons, knot and bury the thread.

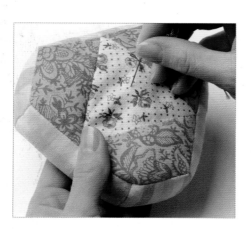

For the outer pockets:

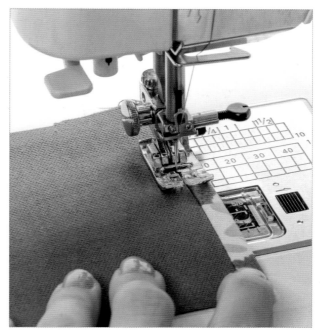

16 Place the lining and main fabric outer side pocket pieces right sides together, aligning the raw edges, and stitch across one short side with a ¼in (6mm) seam.

17 Wrap the lining fabric over the seam and behind the main fabric. Topstitch just under the lining fabric to make an edge of 'trim'. Repeat steps 16 and 17 with the remaining side pocket pieces.

18 Fold one of the main fabric side pieces in half lengthways, then press to crease.

19 Place one pocket right side up on the right side of the side piece, and pin at the top and bottom to hold it in place.

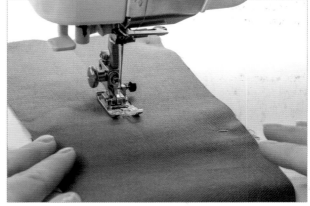

20 From the underside, machine stitch a line up the centre, following the crease, to split the pocket in two. Pin the second pocket right side up on the right side of the remaining side piece but do not split the pocket. Using the template, trace and then cut a curve at the bottom of each side piece and mark the centre.

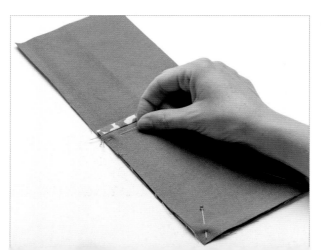

For the bag construction:

21 Take the main fabric body of the bag and make a small crease at the centre of each of the long sides.

22 Starting at the top, pin the body of the bag to one of the side pieces, right sides together and matching the creases at the bottom of the bag. Gradually ease the bag body along the curve. There will be puckers, but you can flatten them out when you stitch the pieces together.

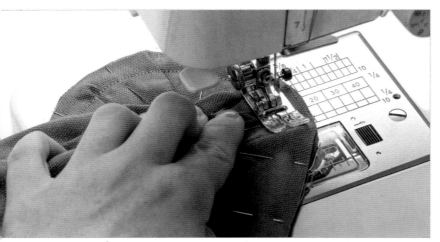

23 Sew the body to one side with a ½in (1cm) seam allowance. Mark and pin the second side, then sew as before.

24 Fold the inside pocket in half lengthways, right sides together. Stitch ¼in (6mm) from the edge on the two short sides.

25 Turn the pocket right side out and press. Topstitch ½in (1cm) from the folded edge.

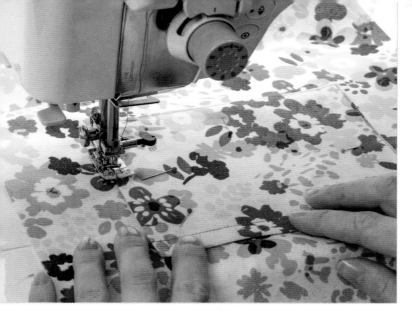

26 Fold under the raw edge by about ¼in (6mm) and press. Position the pocket 2½in (6.5cm) down from the top of one side of the lining and pin in place. Topstitch along three sides, ⅛in (3mm) from the edge and taking a few extra stitches at the two top corners.

27 Mark and pin the body of the lining and sides as you did with the main fabric part of the bag. Sew the body and side panel lining pieces together, leaving a 5in (13cm) gap along one seam to turn the bag through when assembling.

28 Turn the main fabric bag body right side out. Turn the lining wrong side out. Put the main fabric bag into the lining so the right sides are together. Slip the strap in between the two layers and pin in place. Slide the top flap between the layers and pin in place. Leave an extra ½in (1cm) of the flap and strap protruding from the bag body (for a total 1in [2.5cm] seam allowance on these pieces).

Assembling

When you tuck the outer bag into the lining to assemble, the matching fabrics – the lining of the flap and the straps – should face the lining of the bag (front to front). Insert the bag body so that the split pocket ends up on the side you want it – I prefer it at the back (left side when looking at the bag head on).

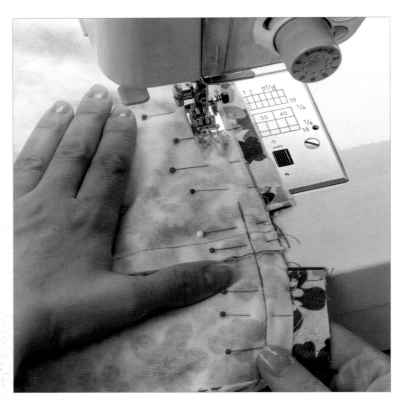

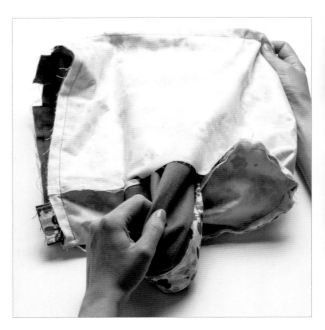

30 Reach into the gap you left in the lining and find the strap. Gently pull the bag parts through the hole and turn right side out. Press the seams well.

29 Stitch around the entire bag, ½in (1cm) from the edge and paying special attention to the backstitch along the flap edges and straps.

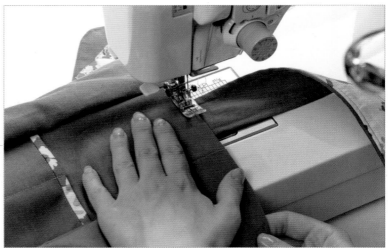

31 Fold in the seam allowance along the gap left in the lining and sew shut close to the edge. Push the lining into the bag.

32 Topstitch the opening and fill the bag with your next EPP project.

Pouches like this have been a staple in Japanese quilting circles for decades. This is the perfect beginner's project – small enough to try out new patterns, yet brilliantly useful once completed. After making this project, why not choose another design from the English paper-piecing patterns chapter (see pages 128–137) and test it out on another little pouch?

Small pouch

For templates, see pages 138–139

1in (2.5cm)
Half hexagon x 50

Top of pouch x 1

Dimensions and specs

The EPP section measures 8 x 11¼in (20 x 28.5cm).

Tools & materials

At least 50 x 1in (2.5cm) half hexagon templates **1**

One or more deep-blue solids, for 36 half hexagons **2**

Assorted prints and coordinating fabrics totalling 36 half hexagons **3**

Two strips of bias binding, 1¼ x 12in (3 x 30cm) **4**

12 x 16in (30 x 40cm) piece of backing fabric **5**

9 x 12½in (23 x 31cm) piece of cotton wadding **6**

Two strips of 1¼ x 3in (3 x 7.5cm) coordinating fabric for tags **7**

8in (20cm) zip **8**

Sewing kit (thimble, straight pins, thread, needle threader, scissors) **9**

Temporary spray adhesive **10**

Acrylic quilter's ruler **11**

Paper and pencil **12**

1 Cut the fabrics and tack to the templates (see pages 36–39).

2 Assemble into nine rows of eight half hexagons.

3 Press the EPP top and remove the edge templates.

4 Layer, tack with spray adhesive and quilt the EPP panel, taking care not to go beyond the edge of the top.

5 Make the tags by folding in ¼in (6mm) on each of the long sides and pressing, then fold the entire piece in half and press again.

6 Trace the template on page 138 on to paper, cut out and draw around at each short end of your quilted piece to mark the curve at the top of the pouch.

7 Cut along the curves.

8 With right sides together, aligning the raw edges, pin the binding in place along each curved end in turn and stitch by hand or machine.

9 Fold the binding over to the wrong side, tuck under ¼in (6mm), pin and stitch to the lining on both sides.

10 Fold the piece right sides together, then mark and sew each side, securing the tags at either end.

11 Trim the excess wadding.

12 Fold the excess lining fabric over the seam allowances and whipstitch by hand.

13 Fold the corners of the pouch into triangles and mark a stitching line 1¾in (4.5cm) from the point. Stitch by machine.

14 Open the zip, tuck the raw edge in and pin to the inside of the pouch. The zip teeth should line up with the top edge of the binding.

15 Stitch one side by hand with backstitch, then the other, tucking in the edges and tail. Use the line of the woven fabric as a guide.

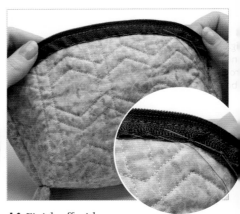

16 Finish off with herringbone stitch (see opposite) along the bottom edge of the zip tape to keep it secure.

Herringbone stitch

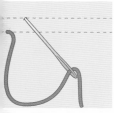

1 Working from the left and on two parallel sewing lines, bring the needle to the surface on the lower sewing line.

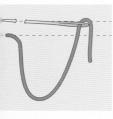

2 Insert the needle a stitch length to the right on the upper sewing line and make a small horizontal stitch from right to left. Keep the thread below the needle.

3 Move a stitch length to the right on the lower sewing line and make a small horizontal stitch from right to left. Keep the thread above the needle.

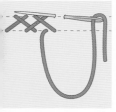

4 Continue forming these two stitches to complete the work.

9 Machine stitch around the edge, following the markings of the tapered edges and leaving a 5in (13cm) opening along one of the long sides.

10 Trim ¼in (6mm) away from the stitched line.

11 Turn the entire piece right side out through the opening in the side and press the edge. Fold under and stitch closed the opening used to turn the project.

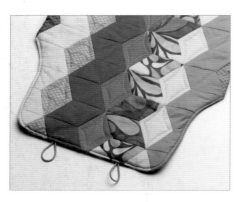

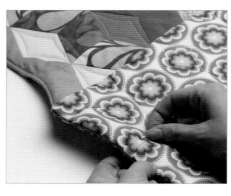

12 Machine quilt the entire piece, taking care not to cross over the edge.

13 Fold the piece with right sides together. Mark and pin a stitching line.

14 Stitch by machine with a ¼in (6mm) seam allowance, backstitching at the opening.

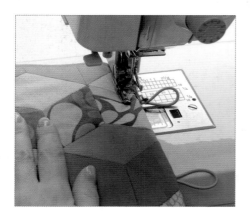

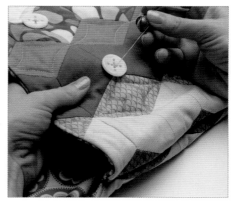

15 Topstitch around the edge of the flap.

16 Turn the piece right side out. Tuck in your laptop to measure where the buttons should go.

17 Stitch the buttons on by hand.

This quilt would look lovely hanging on the wall above a cot in the nursery, and you will have great pleasure hand stitching it while waiting for baby to arrive. The versatile 60-degree diamond and two-colour scheme fit together perfectly in this bright and modern baby quilt. The quilt uses surrounded stars and chain units to create an illusion of stars falling across a night sky.

Falling stars baby quilt

For template, see page 139

1½in (4cm) 60-degree diamond

Dimensions

5½ stars × 8 rows, with diamonds added along the vertical edges to smooth them out.

EPP section measures 29 × 37½in (74 × 95cm)

Entire quilt finishes at 38 × 47in (96.5 × 119cm)

Tools & materials

At least 60 × 1½in (4cm) 60-degree diamond templates **1**

Assorted deep-blue/purple fabric totalling 2yd (1.8m) – choose at least 12 prints **2**

Assorted chartreuse fabric for the stars totalling ⅓yd (28cm) **3**

1¼yd (1.1m) border fabric **4**

1½yd (1.4m) backing fabric **5**

180in (4.6m) double-fold bias binding **6**

Cot-sized wadding (45 × 60in/ 1.1 × 1.5m) **7**

Sewing kit (thimble paper clips, scissors) **8**

Tacking thread **9**

1 Cut your fabric:

a. For the background fabric: 38 × 47in (96.5 × 119cm) rectangle and set aside. Use a portion of the rest of the fabric to cut into diamonds for the centre part of the quilt.

b. For all other fabric: 65 chartreuse diamonds and 465 deep-blue diamonds.

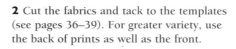

2 Cut the fabrics and tack to the templates (see pages 36–39). For greater variety, use the back of prints as well as the front.

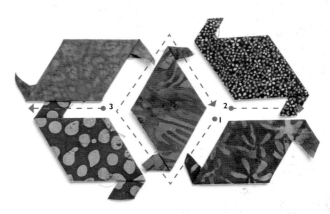

3 Assemble the stars and chain units following the stitch sequences. Surround each star with six deep-blue diamonds. Repeat for the remaining stars, arranging the colours of the diamonds as indicated in the illustration below.

4 Assemble the quilt into eight columns of five stars and one chain unit each, as shown above. The diamonds at the left and right edges of each star are added in step 5.

5 Smooth the edge of the EPP top by adding more deep-blue/purple diamonds.

6 Press the quilt top and remove the edge templates.

7 Press the edge, carefully folding under the seam tails. Tack along the entire outer edge.

8 Position the English paper-pieced part on top of the border and measure with a clear ruler to centre it. Pin in place.

9 Appliqué by hand or machine (see page 49).

10 Flip the quilt top over and from the underside, carefully make an incision in the background fabric about 2in (5cm) inside your machine-appliqué line.

11 Very carefully, being mindful not to cut through the EPP portion, cut out a large rectangle from the background fabric, keeping it just about 2in (5cm) inside the narrowest points of the machine-appliqué line. This will allow for less bulk in your finished quilt. Layer and tack your finished top and quilt as desired. Attach the binding (see pages 54–55).

Piece up a bold section of English paper piecing and then add machine-pieced sections, creating a throw-sized quilt that demands attention. This puzzle piece is made of two diamonds attached to two squares. The shape reminds me of the head of a tanuki, an animal native to Japan and popular in Japanese folklore.

Tanuki stripe throw

For templates, see page 139

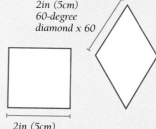

2in (5cm)
60-degree
diamond x 60

2in (5cm)
Square x 60

Dimensions

The EPP section measures 17¾ x 70in (45 x 178cm) .

Completed top measures 55 x 70in (140 x 178cm).

Tools & materials

At least 60 x 2in (5cm) 60-degree diamond templates **1**

At least 60 x 2in (5cm) square templates **2**

Assorted fabrics for the English paper-piecing section, totalling 2yd (1.8m) **3**

Assorted strips for the machine-pieced section, totalling 2½yd (2.3m); use at least 10 fabrics for good variety **4**

4½yd (4.1m) backing fabric **5**

152in (3.8m) bias binding **6**

72 x 90in (1.8 x 2.3m) wadding **7**

Acrylic quilter's ruler **8**

Sewing kit (thimble, paper clips, scissors) **9**

1 For the machine-pieced section, from neutral fabrics, cutting across the full width of the fabric, cut:

a. 7 x 5½in (14cm) strips
b. 7 x 3½in (9cm) strips
c. 7 x 2½in (6.5cm) strips
Sub-cut all of these strips into 7¾in (19.5cm) and 30½in (77.5cm) lengths.

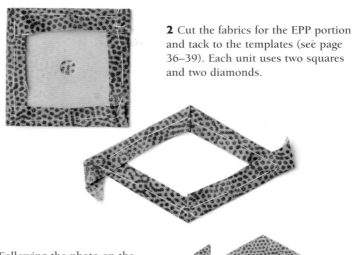

2 Cut the fabrics for the EPP portion and tack to the templates (see page 36–39). Each unit uses two squares and two diamonds.

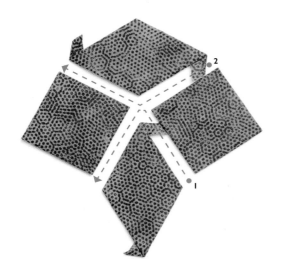

3 Following the photo on the left for the piecing sequence, stitch the unit together, first attaching two squares to the lower diamond and then attaching the top diamond.

4 As you make your tanuki units, join them in groups of five to seven units, and then join the groups together. Piece a column that measures slightly larger than 17¾in (45cm) wide by 73in (185cm) long.

5 Attach extra squares along both long edges of the EPP portion to smooth the edge before cutting.

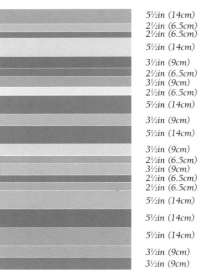

5½in (14cm)
2½in (6.5cm)
2½in (6.5cm)
5½in (14cm)
3½in (9cm)
2½in (6.5cm)
3½in (9cm)
2½in (6.5cm)
5½in (14cm)
3½in (9cm)
5½in (14cm)
3½in (9cm)
2½in (6.5cm)
3½in (9cm)
2½in (6.5cm)
2½in (6.5cm)
5½in (14cm)
5½in (14cm)
5½in (14cm)
3½in (9cm)
3½in (9cm)

6 Lay out the neutral fabric strips that you cut in step 1 in an arrangement that pleases you, using the diagram far left as a guide. Pin and stitch together by machine, ending with a 30½ x 70in (77.5 x 178cm) panel and a smaller 7¾ x 70in (19.5 x 178cm) panel. Be careful not to distort the strips as you piece. Press the seams to one side. Set aside.

7 Remove the edge templates and press the EPP section.

8 With your ruler and rotary cutter, slice a straight line down the entire edge of the piece (long left and right sides only).

9 With right sides together, pin the neutral panels to the left and right of the EPP section. Machine stitch, taking a ¼in (6mm) seam and backstitching the seams of the EPP section as you go. Press the seams away from the EPP section. Again using your ruler and rotary cutter, cut the top and bottom edges of the EPP portion flush with the neutral strips on either side. Layer and tack your finished top and quilt as desired. Attach the binding (see pages 54–55).

Enhance your favourite photos with a custom-made mount. This project is an excellent way to showcase the tiniest of scraps in your collection.

Photo frame

For template, see page 139

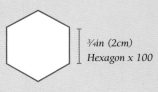

¾in (2cm)
Hexagon x 100

Dimensions

Dimensions of the pieced section depend on the size of your photo frame and mount.

Tools & materials

Photo frame with mount **1**

100 x ¾in (2cm) hexagon templates **2**

Fabric scraps **3**

Spray starch **4**

Temporary spray adhesive or general craft/fabric glue **5**

A favourite photograph **6**

Sewing kit (scissors, thread, needle, paper clips) **7**

Paper **8**

Pencil **10**

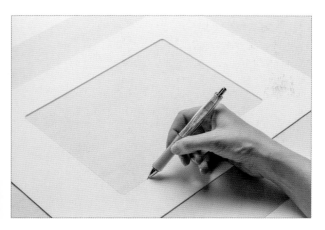

I Trace the mount of a photo frame on to paper.

2 Lay your template pieces on top to fill in the area, making sure that no gaps show through. You may need to cover the lines and make the patchwork mount larger than the original to account for the EPP template size.

3 Count the total templates needed, cut the fabric and tack to the templates (see pages 36–39).

4 Using your paper template, lay out the tacked shapes and play around until you find a pleasing arrangement (see above). Sew them together (see left).

6 Remove the templates carefully, spray with starch and press well.

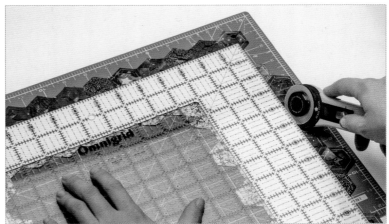

7 Lay the EPP mount face down and position the original mount on top of it. Using the paper mount as a guide, place your acrylic ruler on top and trim the four outer edges only with your rotary cutter.

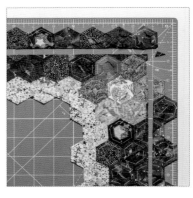

The trimmed edges, step 7

8 Remove the paper mount and the ruler, then transfer the EPP mount, still face down, to a newspaper-covered surface. Apply spray adhesive or glue, then position the EPP portion over the mount and press firmly to attach.

9 Once dry, place the EPP mount in the frame and add your photo. When attaching the frame backing, make sure that the mount is tight against the glass for a snug fit.

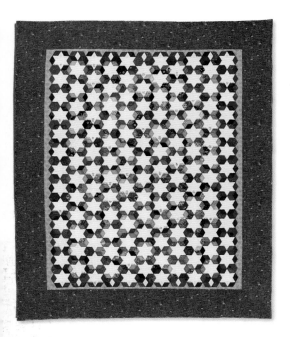

This is the ultimate memory quilt. Carry this project with you wherever you go, and jot down the date and location on each completed star. Capture birthdays, holidays and time spent stitching with friends. Allow the scrappy fabric placement to be random, or planned on impulse – I loved letting my family or friends choose the six coloured diamonds for a star, so that I'd have memories of that visit captured in the quilt as well.

Travel quilt

For template, see page 139

1½in (4cm)
60-degree diamond
x 100

Dimensions

EPP portion measures 51 x 68¼in (130 x 173cm) at the widest points and 50 x 65⅓in (127 x 166cm) at the narrowest points.

Entire quilt finishes at 70 x 86½in (178 x 220cm).

Tools & materials

60-degree diamond templates, 1½in (4cm) per side (depending on your piecing style, you may feel more comfortable with more or fewer, but start with at least 100 templates) **1**

Assorted red fabric for the border stars, totalling 1yd (0.9m) **2**

Assorted fabric for the background, totalling 2½yd (2.3m) **3**

White fabric totalling 3½yd (3.2m) **4**

2½yd (2.3m) fabric for the outer border; more will be required if using fabric with a directional print **5**

¾yd (0.7m) fabric for the inner border **6**

6yd (5.5m) backing fabric **7**

326in (8.2m) binding **8**

Twin-sized wadding, 72 x 90in (183 x 229cm) **9**

Sewing kit (scissors, straight pins, thimble, and thread) **10**

Fine permanent marker **11**

Acrylic ruler and rotary blade **12**

1 Cut the fabrics and tack to the templates (see pages 36–39). For greater variety, use the backs of the prints as well as the front.

2 Assemble six white diamonds into a star, following the stitch sequence. Surround it with six multicoloured diamonds. Repeat for a total of 104 centre units. Assemble six white diamonds into a star. Surround it with six red diamonds. Repeat for a total of 34 border units.

3 Assemble four red diamonds around one white diamond in a chain unit, following the stitch sequence. Repeat for a total of 10 border units for the top and bottom of the quilt.

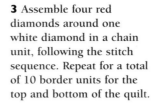
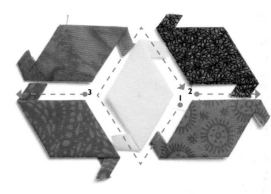

4 As you piece the units, jot down the date and location with a fine permanent marker, either holding the fabric taut or writing on the fabric before you remove the templates.

5 Assemble the quilt into 11 columns of 13 stars each, or 12 stars and 2 chains, as shown.

6 Add red diamonds along the two long edges to smooth them out.

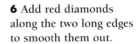

7 Remove the templates and give the edges a good press, tucking the seam tails under as you go (see Assembling and finishing, pages 50–57).

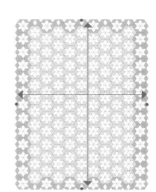

8 Tack the pressed edge with pins or thread (left). Measure your quilt through the centre from the narrowest points (blue lines, right). Add 20in (50cm) to each of the vertical and horizontal measurements to get the correct border lengths, and cut the border fabric. Mark the centres of all four sides with a pin or masking tape (pink dots, right) and match these markings to the ones you'll make on the border to line the two pieces up correctly.

9 With right sides together, pin each inner border strip to an outer border strip, ending with pieces 10¾in (27cm) wide by the length determined in step 8. Machine stitch, with a ¼in (6mm) seam.

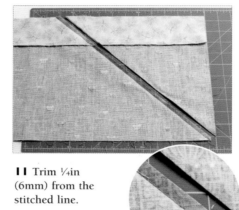

10 To mitre the corners of the border, place two adjacent border pieces right sides together, aligning the seams of the inner border. Measure and draw a 45-degree line from the corner of the outer border fabric to the raw edge of the inner border. Pin and machine stitch on this line.

11 Trim ¼in (6mm) from the stitched line.

12 Press open. Repeat for the remaining three corners. Mark the centres of all four sides with pins or masking tape.

13 Lay the border frame out on a flat surface such as a table or floor, and tape it in place, maintaining the 90-degree angle.

14 Place the EPP portion on top and use pins to tack one quadrant at a time (aligning the pins you used to mark the centres in step 8 and 12), using an acrylic ruler to measure that ½in (1cm) of the border is under the innermost points.

15 Tack and appliqué by hand or machine (see page 49). Layer and tack your finished top and quilt as desired. Attach the binding (see page 54).

chapter 4

English paper-piecing patterns

Now that you understand how easily English paper-pieced patterns can go together, let's look at the possibilities of working with some other shapes and combinations. This chapter has ten puzzle pieces that you can use to create your own portable designs. There is blank graph paper in Chapter 5 (see page 126) for you to try out your own colour schemes.

Hexagons

A simple flower made from seven hexagons is a classic, traditional quilt pattern. Instead of joining six templates of one fabric to make the petals of a flower, use only two or three templates of one fabric and join them to make a fresh pattern. Add extra background hexagons as you join the blocks to space out the puzzle pieces and alter the pattern as you like.

For a larger version of this grid, see page 128

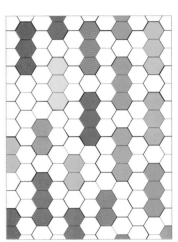

Join the outer ring to the centre hexagon one template at a time, adding the next hexagon and backtracking along the seam allowance (see page 140) before stitching it to the centre. If the fabrics you are using for the background and the dashes contrast strongly, two thread colours and a different piecing sequence may be necessary.

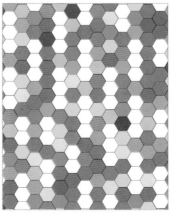

Variations

A. Form multicoloured flowers with a uniform centre for a classic look (see page 44).

B. Try leaving the dashes white and making the background from scraps.

C. Arrange your hexagons in stacked rows, with a solid border around each column.

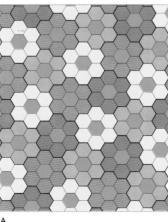

A

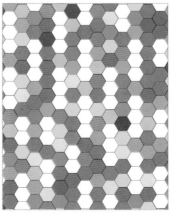

B

C

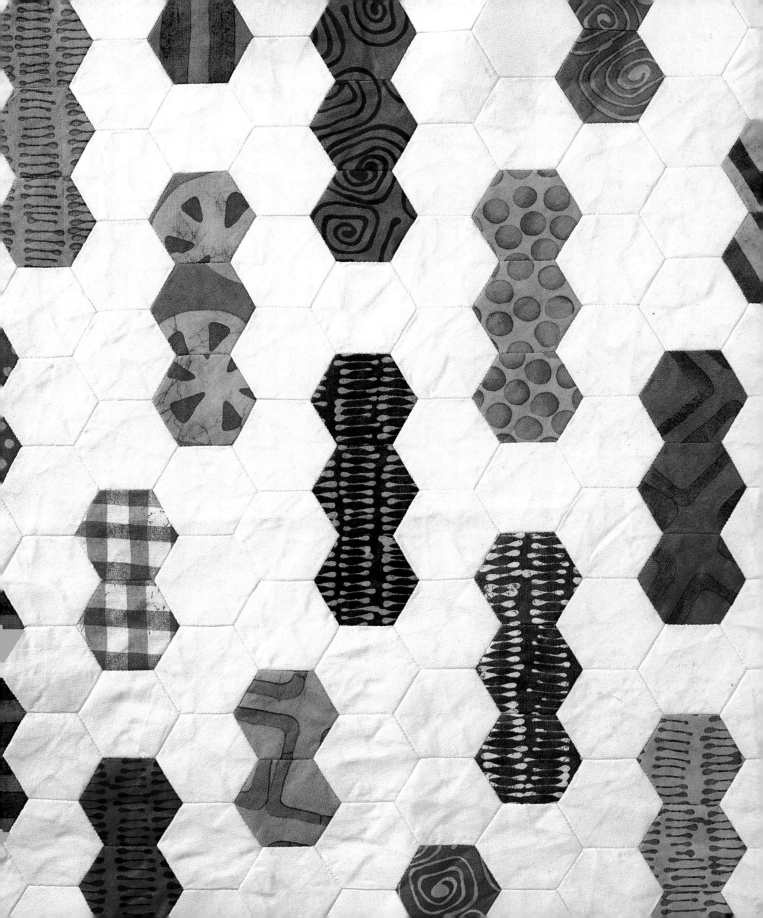

60-degree diamonds with interlocking background

This pattern is a great way to make a pile of random scraps look cohesive and cheerful. Make stars in two tones of the same colour and add two background diamonds for an eight-shape puzzle piece. These puzzle pieces can be rotated to fit with each other as you join them, and extra background pieces can be added as you go.

For a larger version of this grid, see page 129

Start by stitching three diamonds together, dark-light-dark. Then make a three-diamond unit of light-dark-light and add two background pieces before sewing the two halves of the star together.

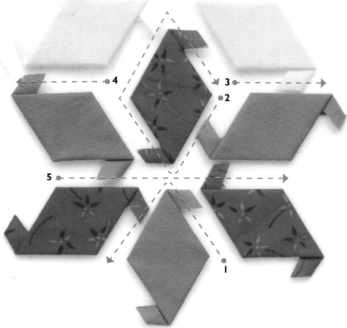

Variations

A. To control the tone of the piece, try making each star from a single fabric. For an excellent example of this pattern, see Lesly Wade-Woolley's piece on page 12.

B. For the ultimate scrap quilt, make white stars and a multicoloured background.

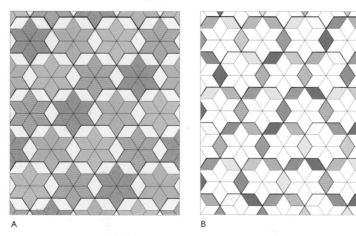

A

B

Half hexagons

Half hexagons are a versatile shape. Here, a basic puzzle-piece unit is done in three background and three print pieces, and the units are stitched together to create the appearance of vertical rows. By following the piecing sequence below, you avoid bending the templates until you start to join puzzle pieces, thereby prolonging the life of your templates.

For a larger version of this grid, see page 130

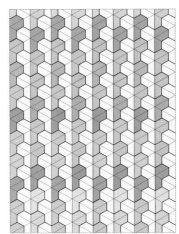

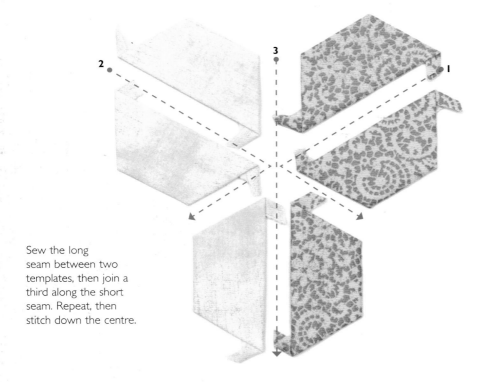

Sew the long seam between two templates, then join a third along the short seam. Repeat, then stitch down the centre.

Variations

A. *Careful placement of light, medium and dark fabrics can create an optical illusion.*

B. *Triangles appear when the puzzle piece is made using alternating light and dark fabrics.*

C. *Go bold and piece each puzzle piece from a single fabric.*

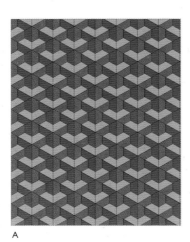

A

B

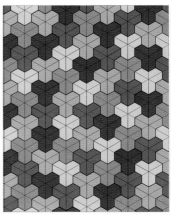

C

60-degree diamonds and squares

Turn your scraps into a striking grid in this pattern that alternates 60-degree diamonds with squares. The puzzle piece is deceptively easy to stitch together and blocks soon start to accumulate. This is a simple pattern that can be transformed multiple times by colour or value placement.

For a larger version of this grid, see page 131

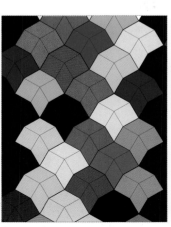

Attach two squares to the acute angle of one diamond, then attach the second diamond across the top.

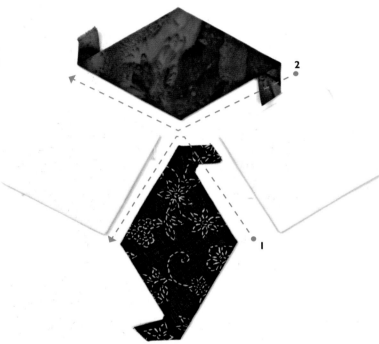

2

1

Variations

A. Careful placement of coloured squares can produce bands of colour across the quilt.

B. Two-tone puzzle pieces are a great way to use up small scraps.

C. Puzzle pieces made from one fabric allow for bolder options with colour play. (See Tanuki Stripe Throw, pages 92–95.)

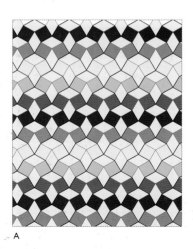

A

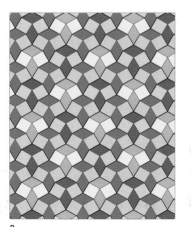

B

C

60-degree diamonds and half hexagons

60- and 120-degree angles playfully float around on this simple pattern made of half hexagons and diamonds. Different colorations completely change the look – try some out and see what works best for you.

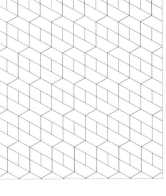

For a larger version of this grid, see page 132

Join two diamonds, then add a half hexagon to either side.

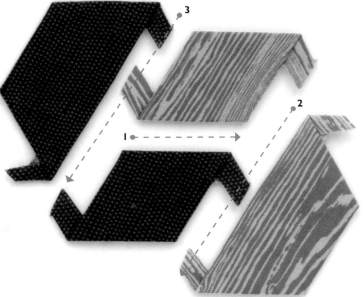

Variations

For the variations, the grid may need to be rotated.

A. Clear out your scrap bin and make a bright and colourful quilt.

B. Changing the colour of half a unit can make little flowers appear.

C. Leave one diamond white and double the units, giving a simple pattern a more complex look.

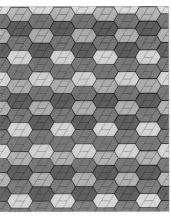

A

B

C

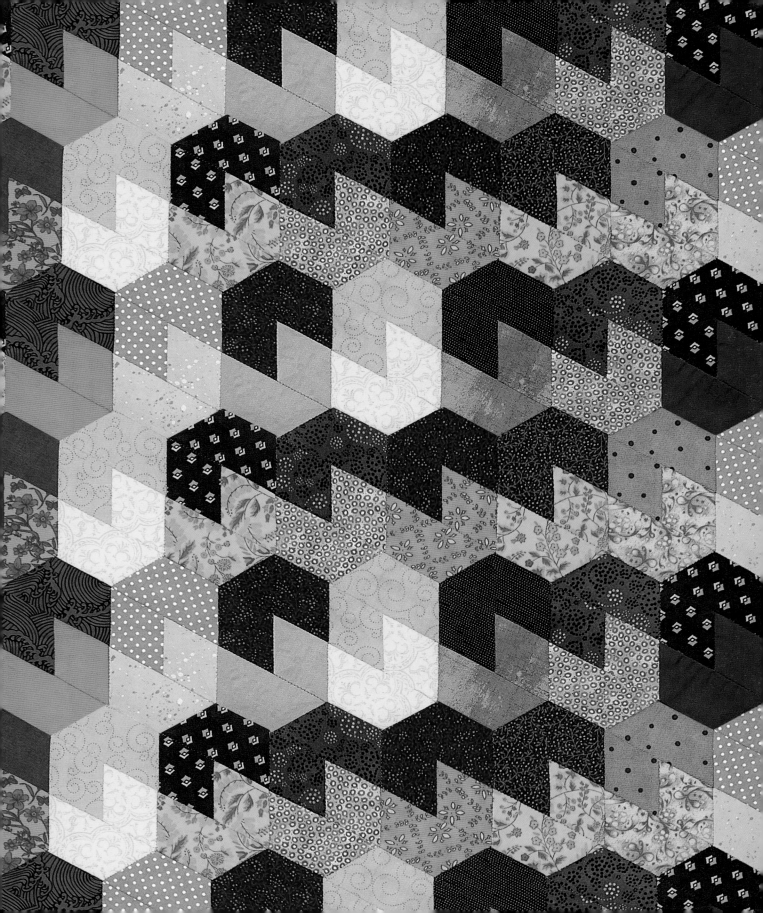

60-degree diamonds and hexagons: flowers and leaves

Grandma's Flower Garden is a traditional English paper-piecing pattern and arguably the best known. By adding some 60-degree diamonds, the flowers gain 'leaves' and the pattern gets a new look. Try flowers of all the same colour, or spread them on a dark background fabric.

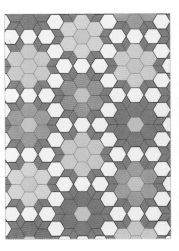

For a larger version of this grid, see page 133

Stitch all petals to the centre, backtracking as you go (see page 140). Stitch the leaves in pairs. Attach them all in one go, without starting and stopping your thread, by hiding the thread in the seam allowance of the flowers as you jump from one pair of leaves to the next.

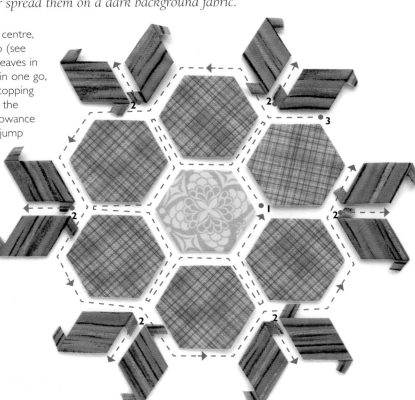

Variations

A. Combine a bunch of fabrics in the same shade to give your monochrome scrappy flowers more interest.

B. Single-coloured flowers on a dark background have a bold impact.

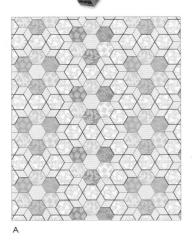

A

B

60-degree diamonds and hexagons: elongated hexagons

For a larger version of this grid, see page 134

Stack two hexagons and add a diamond at either side to make an elongated hexagon that can be coloured and shaded to create more complex patterns.

Start by stitching a diamond, then a hexagon and then the remaining diamond to three sides of the top hexagon. Finish by stitching the remaining seams.

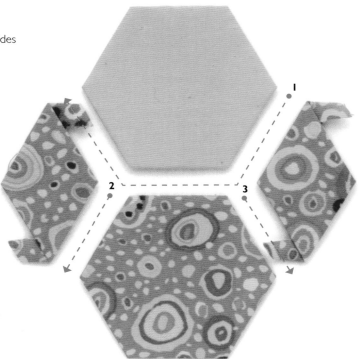

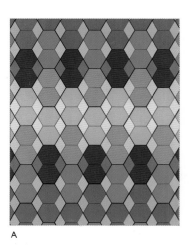

Variations

A. Give balance to your quilt top by stitching two-tone puzzle pieces.

B. Calm your scraps into rows of dark and light diamonds.

C. Display your stash and make each puzzle piece from a separate fabric.

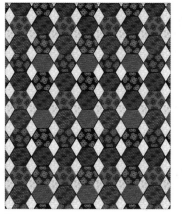

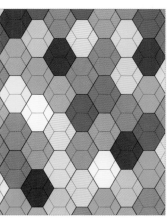

A

B

C

Hexagons and half hexagons

Careful placement of four half hexagons around the sides of one hexagon creates a diamond that can be shaded and played with until you find a pattern that speaks to you. In this sample, bright arrows dart across the quilt top on a background of grey.

For a larger version of this grid, see page 135

Add four half hexagons to one hexagon, backtracking the side seams as you go (see page 140).

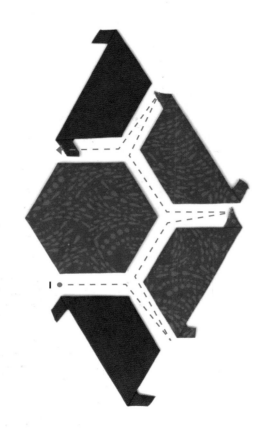

Variations

A. Keep one shape the same colour in all units, and set the units in rows of colour across your quilt.

B. Turn the pattern slightly and you can make fish swim in a sea of blue.

C. Rotate the puzzle piece and an entirely new pattern emerges.

A

B

C

Equilateral triangles and squares

Equilateral triangles can be joined with squares to create simple yet intricate-looking patterns of stars, hearts and stripes. An ambitious quilter may even want to design a quilt combining all of these motifs, which can easily be done with a sheet of graph paper and determination.

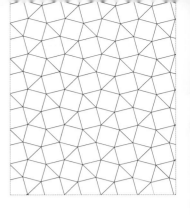

For a larger version of this grid, see page 136

Attach four triangles to a square. Add filler squares as you piece the units together.

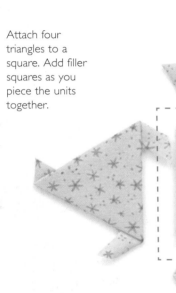

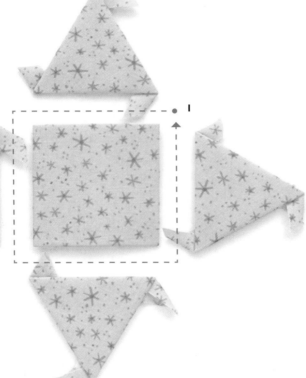

Variations

For the variations, the grid may need to be rotated.

A. Make a puzzle piece with only three templates, and a pattern of interlocking hearts appears.

B. Play with values and add triangles in two tones to a dark square.

C. Vertical stripes make a bold statement.

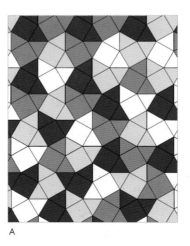

A

B

C

Hexagons, equilateral triangles and squares

For a larger version of this grid, see page 137

The more shapes you add, the more complex your design options become. Here, three shapes are combined to make bright, two-toned circles play across the surface of the quilt. Easily pieced in units and then added to the puzzle shape, this pattern works up quickly.

First, stitch a triangle to each of the squares, then stitch the squares around the centre hexagon. Pop out the template and go back to stitch the remaining side seams.

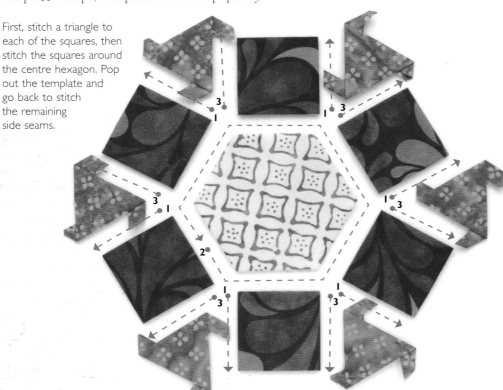

Variations

A. Limit your palette to three colours and see new shapes appear.

B. Careful colour placement around the puzzle piece makes horizontal stripes of colour appear.

C. Make some colourful puzzle shapes and set them floating on a plain background.

A

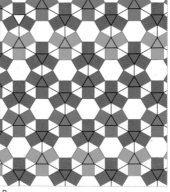

B

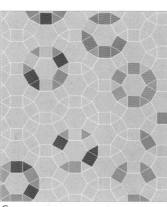

C

5

chapter

Paper-piecing resources

In this chapter, you will find all types of resources to guide and help you become a confident English paper piecer. Want to try out your own patterns? Grab some coloured pencils and flip to the grid of your choice. Just start playing and see where your intuition takes you. Ready to shop for fabric and templates? My favourite retailers are listed at the back of the book.

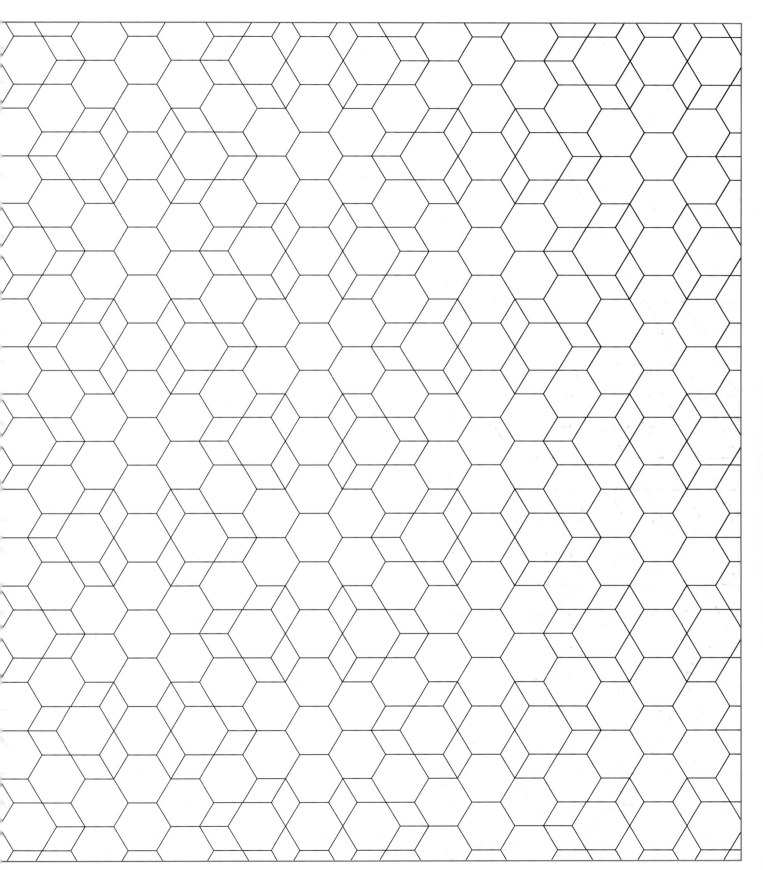

Templates

Project templates

The dotted line down the centre of the templates indicates the centre of the pattern. Enlarge these templates by 200%, cut them out and use them to get the correct shape of the pattern indicated.

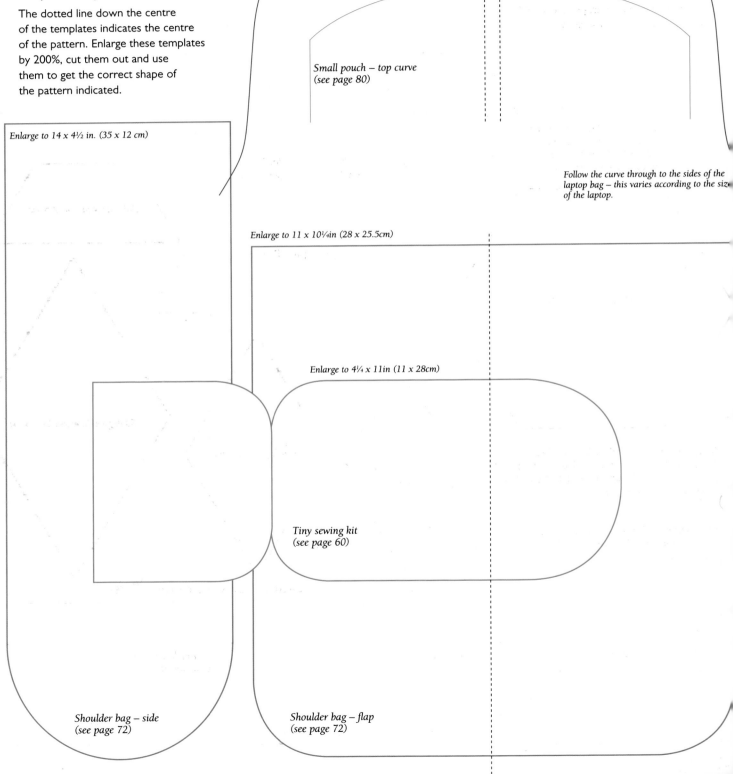

Laptop bag – flap
(see page 84)

Small pouch – top curve
(see page 80)

Enlarge to 14 x 4½ in. (35 x 12 cm)

Follow the curve through to the sides of the laptop bag – this varies according to the size of the laptop.

Enlarge to 11 x 10¼in (28 x 25.5cm)

Enlarge to 4¼ x 11in (11 x 28cm)

Tiny sewing kit
(see page 60)

Shoulder bag – side
(see page 72)

Shoulder bag – flap
(see page 72)

Credits

Author acknowledgements

This book would not have been possible without the help of many minds and hands. I would first like to thank my husband for his love, patience and support, and my sons for keeping me company as I stitched. I love you guys.

To anyone who has sat with me as I have quilted – thank you for accepting me for who I am.

To all of the quilters who have shared knowledge, laughter and fabric scraps, especially Kikuyo Kubota and Helen Thompson.

To the NYC Metro Modern Quilt Guild, for giving me the community of inspiration and laughter that I had searched for.

Special thanks to Victoria Findlay Wolfe and the guild officers for permission to use the guild blog images on page 13, and to Nicole Kaplan, David Sisson, Mary Bakija, Cassandra Rosser, Christa Farmer and Earamichia Brown for being part of the photo shoot in Central Park, page 11.

To my English paper piecers, without whom I would have never finished all the projects and samples in the book: Merrill Rosenberg (who first suggested I write a book on EPP) for brainstorming ideas, testing patterns, helping with photo shoots, keeping me motivated, focused, and inspired, and contributing to the sample, page 119; Becky Lovasz for contributing to the Tanuki stripe throw, page 95, and the Falling stars quilt, page 91, also for the use of her quilt on pages 44, 45 and 47; Christa Farmer for contributing to the Laptop bag, page 87; Earamichia Brown for contributing to the sample, page 119; Bernadette Forward for contributing to the samples, pages 119 and 121; Helen Beall for contributing to the Laptop bag, page 87; Shannon Couvillion for stitching the sample, page 115, as well as for her amazing long-arm skills on both the Travel quilt, page 103, and Falling stars quilt, page 91.

Lesly Wade-Woolley for permission to use her quilt, pages 12, 26, 57, 126.

Clare O'Rourke for permission to use her quilt, page 48.

Thank you to my editor, Katie Crous, as well as Ruth Patrick, Jackie Palmer and Kate Kirby, and the rest of the dedicated team at Quarto.

My photographer, Ned Witrogen.

Moda Fabrics for their generous contribution of fabrics for book projects, and Pati Shambaugh at Picking Up the Pieces for creating Quilt Patis templates and generously contributing packs of all sizes for the projects in this book.

Dedication:
For my parents. Thank you for your unwavering belief in my dreams.

References:
200 Quilting Tips, Techniques & Trade Secrets Susan Briscoe
The Encyclopedia of Quilting Techniques Katharine Guerrier

Publisher acknowledgements

Quarto would like to thank:

Moda Fabrics for supplying fabrics for book projects.

Francesca Carslake, p.99r